COLD WAR CANDLES

CANDLES

Adventures Of A Seventies Seafarer

For Davinia.
I hope you enjoy reading this as much
as I did writing it!
                                    Nick

Nick Eliason

MAPLE
PUBLISHERS

Cold War Candles

Author: Nick Eliason

Copyright © Nick Eliason (2022)

The right of Nick Eliason to be identified as author of this work has been asserted by the author in accordance with section 77 and 78 of the Copyright, Designs and Patents Act 1988.

First Published in 2022

ISBN 978-1-915164-96-4 (Paperback)

Book cover design and Book layout by:
  White Magic Studios
  www.whitemagicstudios.co.uk

Published by:
  Maple Publishers
  1 Brunel Way,
  Slough,
  SL1 1FQ, UK
  www.maplepublishers.com

CONTENTS

Cold War Candles
Adventures Of A Seventies Seafarer

E xpelled from his grammar school in 1971, the author desperately sought an escape from the direction that life was taking him. The threat of working hard in an Israeli kibbutz without pay for the next year didn't appeal, but an advertisement in a Sunday newspaper did. The British Shipping Federation was offering opportunities to make a career in the Merchant Navy.

Knowing nothing of ships and seafaring, an application was nonetheless submitted which resulted in unexpected acceptance. A year at sea might enable a more suitable career choice to be made.

However, an unforgettable era was just beginning.

For the next ten years, seafaring heralded a series of adventures for a deck cadet who rose to become a second mate during a period of slow decline for the British merchant navy.

Experiencing life aboard all types of merchant ship, including a spell on Queen Elizabeth Two, there was always adventure on hand. This account is a chronological description of those experiences, compiled from contemporary records, letters, documents and photographs.

The author's career culminated in an audacious quest to venture behind the Iron Curtain in an attempt to marry a Soviet citizen. An unlikely, and ill-advised, relationship had developed during visits to the U.S.S.R.

The writing style is intended to be concise and fast-paced to maintain a casual reader's interest.

I hope this has been achieved.

Nick Eliason.

Chapter 1

Mr Burrage's Kibbutz

My last year at Alleyne's Grammar School in Stevenage didn't turn out well.

I returned for the autumn term of 1971 expecting to continue my chosen subjects in the sixth form. My headmaster, Mr Burrage had other ideas. It would appear that I had become a part of what he considered 'the wrong crowd'. Along with half a dozen of my friends, I was accused of engaging in disruptive tactics and as a result 'needed to be made an example of'.

My father was summoned to Mr Burrage's study one evening where a discussion took place in my absence. Later that same evening when my dad returned home, I could tell he was not happy. In no uncertain terms he told me that I was not returning to school anymore.

I was ecstatic! However, the feeling didn't last long - I had been expelled.

Expelled! Me! Not possible! There may have been some weak grounds for such a draconian decision, but expulsion was, in my mind, an over-reaction.

Mr Burrage had sold to my father the idea that I should spend the next year on a kibbutz.

What on earth was a kibbutz? Apparently, at this time, young people from all over the world could apply to live in an enclosed community, work together in harmony and become totally self-sufficient. In Israel. It was trendy. Young people would learn to become responsible adults.

Fine. I was happy with the idea of foreign travel and meeting like-minded young people. Some of my school friends had already begun jobs which paid a decent wage. They had become independent and I had become rather envious.

My dad was happy with the idea of me being away for a year - or two.

So how much money could I expect to earn on such an enterprise in a year - or two?

Nothing. These trendy communities worked on the principle that being self-sufficient by producing their own food and living accommodation rendered money unnecessary.

Trendy it may have been, but I wanted to be paid for being trendy.

So began my desperate search for an alternative that would get me away from home and earning money at the same time. In this case, communism would be defeated by capitalism.

That very weekend, I was scanning the 'situations vacant' section of a Sunday broadsheet newspaper when my gaze was drawn to an advertisement placed by the British Shipping Federation. There was an illustration of a ship's officer walking up the gangway of a huge vessel.

I don't quite remember the caption but it impressed me. It got me thinking. A career at sea?

My home was in Knebworth, about as far from the sea as it is possible to be in the U.K.

I didn't know anyone who had been in The Merchant Navy. I didn't know anything about ships, although I did have a poster on my bedroom wall illustrating different types.

In an effort to divert my dad's ongoing plans for my imminent departure to Israel, I discussed the advertisement I had seen with him. His enthusiasm was obvious. So much so, that he began to regale me with stories about his grandad who had spent his lifetime at sea. A fact I never knew.

A coupon that accompanied the advertisement was duly completed and posted.

Amazingly, I received a reply within a few days. I was now invited to The British Shipping Federation offices in London for interview. My dad was really pleased and even offered to come with me. Maybe he just wanted to make sure I arrived for the interview. In any case, the small matter of my expulsion from school was not mentioned again.

On the appointed day, I arrived in Prescot Street in plenty of time. I would be there for eight hours.

I never expected exams! First maths and then English. I had 'O levels' in both but the selection board had set standards of their own. These tests took up the morning. My answer sheets were whisked away for scrutiny before a break for lunch.

During the lunch break I had the opportunity to talk to other aspiring seafarers who had answered the call. Almost all had family backgrounds steeped in maritime history. What was I doing here?

That afternoon, I was subjected to a series of interviews. The last of these was conducted by a man sporting a full set of facial hair to match his rugged features. The thought went through my mind that he could have made a second living advertising fish fingers. Following a lengthy dialogue, he finished by asking:

"If successful, what sort of shipping company would you be looking to sail with, young man?"

I had no idea - but I had recently read Alistair Maclean's novel 'The Golden Rendezvous' in which a merchant ship named 'Campari' was the central focus. 'Campari' was a passenger-cargo ship.

"My first choice would be passenger-cargo ships." I unhesitatingly replied.

"I see. And in what capacity - deck, engineer, radio or catering?"

I had no idea - but the hero of the novel was a chief officer.

"I would eventually like to make chief officer" I said with great enthusiasm.

"Well, why not captain, you certainly seem to have strong ambitions."

My interviewer didn't wait for an answer but instead told me that he would be recommending me for further interview with Port Line. He was at pains to point out that in his opinion, Port Line was the finest passenger-cargo shipping company in the British Merchant Navy and furthermore, its officers were the very best.

Blimey! What had I started? An exciting, but extremely uncertain future by the look of it.

If I was making a mistake, I could always blame Alistair Maclean.

Chapter 2

Captain Paton's Interview

My rail journey to London on the 13th of December 1971 was clouded by apprehension. I had been invited for interview at the hallowed halls of the Port Line Shipping Company following referral by The British Shipping Federation.

I still knew almost nothing about ships or the role of a deck officer in the merchant navy. My search in the local library had drawn a blank, and all I had for reference was the wall chart in my bedroom and a dusty old book relating to the days of sail. However, I now knew that my great-grandad had been the first mate on a famous sailing ship. I completely read the only book I had.

The Herzogin Cecilie was a windjammer sailing ship of the early twentieth century. She was renowned for her speed and made her name during the races to transport grain cargoes from Australia to the U.K. I had been told, during an uncharacteristic conversation with my dad, that his own grandad had been the chief officer of that very ship, and furthermore, had lost a hand in a rigging accident. He was also aboard when she came to grief during heavy fog off the south Devon coast. The whole incident was well documented at the time and the crew were revered by seafarers worldwide. They were the rock-stars of their generation. Enthralling stuff, I thought.

The man who greeted me rather cooly in the interview room introduced himself as Captain Paton. He had the appearance of a character who may have spent many of his years exposing his face to wind, sun and rain. He was an impressive figure and I began to feel nervous.

Captain Paton sat back in the chair he was occupying behind a vast wooden desk, and indicated that I could sit on the chair in front of him. He took a pipe from the desk top and spent an exaggerated amount of time cleaning, filling and then lighting it. Most of this time was spent looking directly at me which I found rather uncomfortable. He then spent more time scrutinising a piece of paper that he picked up, all the while puffing away heavily on the pipe.

The conversation that followed began fairly predictably, being questions that focused on my education and interests. These were easily answered but I still felt under interrogation. Then I was asked if I was from a sea-faring family. The short answer would have been negative but at least I was able to mention my great-grandad. On hearing the name Herzogin Cecilie, Captain Paton's eyes lit up and he even removed the pipe from his mouth.

"Herzogin Cecilie you say?" He went on, "**The** Herzogin Cecilie?"

I related at length what I had been told about this famous ship and my great-grandad's equally famous contribution to maritime history.

After listening to what I had to say, the captain confided in me that he had a special interest in the sailing ships of that era and knew well the story of great-grandad's ship.

The interview was then concluded quite abruptly. No more questions. I wondered what was coming next as the interrogation hadn't even touched on details of the job I had applied for.

"Well, said Captain Paton. You seem to be the sort of young chap we're looking for. I'm going to recommend you for a cadetship with us, starting right away. We will get a letter of confirmation in this afternoon's post. I'm sure your great-grandad would be proud of your serving with Port Line."

We shook hands and that was it. The secretary outside Captain Paton's office offered her congratulations while handing me a booklet entitled 'So you're going to sea'.

I studied the cover of the booklet and felt pleased with myself. "Looks like it now" I thought.

The train journey home was accompanied by a strong feeling of relief and excitement. My future started to look bright. The little book was inspiring but only answered a few basic questions. I wondered, what would life really be like on ships? Would I be seasick? Would I be up to the job?

I still have that little booklet.

When I arrived home, my dad was already waiting to hear a full account on the day's events. He was genuinely pleased that I had passed the interview and been offered a cadetship. I told him that I believed the success of the day had been in no small part due to great-grandad's adventures aboard the Herzogin Cecilie that he had recounted.

My dad looked thoughtful and then quietly muttered: "Did I say the Herzogin Cecilie? Of course it may well have been some other ship - but he went to sea - I am sure of that!"

Postscript: No evidence has yet surfaced that my great-grandad, Christopher Eliason, ever set foot aboard such a ship. On the day the Herzogin Cecilie went aground, the 25th of April 1936, she was commanded by a Sven Erikson and the first mate was Elis Karlsson.

I conclude that my sea-faring career was founded on misinformation.

Blue Star Port Lines (Management) Limited

14 Fenchurch Avenue London EC3M 5JS

Telegrams Overseas BLUEPORT LONDON EC3 **Inland** BLUEPORT LONDON TELEX
Telephone 01-700 1891 Telex 886109

01 488 4567   Our Reference   DAH/BWL   Your Reference

13th December 1971

Mr. N.J. Eliason,
3, Deards Wood,
Knebworth,
Herts.

Dear Sir,

Further to your interview with Captain Paton this morning, I would confirm, that you have been accepted for a future Navigating Cadetship with Port Line, with your being on salary of £39.75 per month as from 1.1.72.

I would further confirm, that it is intended to enrol you with the School of Navigation, Warsash, with my repeating, that it will be to the School's discretion as to whether you follow an O.N.C. or O.N.D. Course. Meanwhile, as explained, Warsash will be contacting you shortly as regards all necessary formalities, and, attending their own entrance interview/examination. All travelling expenses incurred, will, of course, be refunded to you.

I would further confirm, that as and when you have to attend Warsash, it is necessary you also attend the Shipping Federation Office in Southampton (19/23 Canute Road) to undergo their standard New Entrants Medical/Opthalmic Examination. I am advising the Medical Officer that you will be coming, but would ask you to telephone him (Southampton 23546) once you know when you will be in Southampton.

Finally, I would repeat that between now and the 1st January, you must open a current Bank Account and then complete and return the enclosed 'Offsal' form to this office, together with your National Insurance Card. Now, however, will you please acknowledge receipt of this letter; whilst should you find yourself in any difficulties or, have any queries, please do not hesitate to contact me.

Yours faithfully,
BLUE STAR/PORT LINES (MANAGEMENT) LTD.

D.A. Hume
Personnel Officer
Marine Superintendents Department

Directors E.H. Vestey *Chairman*   B.R. Hazlitt D.G. Hollebone MBE MC TD J.G. Payne W.B. Slater N.S. Thompson

Acceptance

Chapter 3

Warsash

Situated on the lower east bank of the River Hamble in Hampshire, just outside the village of Warsash, was the grandly titled: University Of Southampton School Of Navigation.

Port Line had enrolled me here for a start date of 6th of January 1972.

I arrived along with nineteen potential navigators from other, mainly British, shipping companies.

From the guard room adjacent to the main gate, we were shown to an accommodation block at the far end of the building complex. It was a relief to discover our lodgings were of newer build than the string of buildings around the guard house. The site had been part of HMS Tormentor, a Royal Marines training base until 1946, when it became the Southampton School of Navigation, a satellite of Southampton University.

The accommodation block consisted of four floors, the first three being sub-divided into houses named after famous explorers: Hudson, Shackleton and Wilson. The top floor was intended for recreation. On this floor, at each end, was an open balcony that overlooked Southampton Water.

The rooms we were allocated were referred to as 'cabins'. Each cabin featured six bunk beds, a large table and a personal locker. There was a window at each end of the room and a corridor leading to washing facilities. On our first day, we were allowed to settle in and get acquainted with our room-mates. We were all curious to discover what lay in store over the next three months.

We soon found out. Our first full day comprised yet another series of examinations. Maths, English and General Science were on the menu. Perhaps the school wanted to filter any imposters from the course at an early stage. Anyway, once the answer papers had been checked, I was offered an O.N.C. course in Nautical Science. This would be in addition to training for the Second Mate's Certificate of Competency. It was naturally expected that I would remain studying for both qualifications for the four year duration. Besides, my dad was willing to sign an agreement to that effect and rendered himself as surety.

Now that expectation put me on the spot. The whole 'going to sea' enterprise was, in my mind, simply a means to escape exile to an Israeli kibbutz. I reckoned that a year travelling the world on ships would be far preferable to a year spent picking oranges. I would get paid too!

On our second day we had a full tour of the campus. Most of the buildings were purpose-built during the 1960's, so appeared very modern compared to the remaining Royal Navy edifices.

In addition to a teaching block, there was a large library, offices, refectory with bar area, and down on the foreshore, past a parade ground with sundry huts, was a large boathouse with a pier that extended out into the River Hamble.

By day three, a 'uniform' was ready for issue. This comprised a thick blue cotton shirt, blue woollen pullover with embroidered name badge, dark grey trousers and a Royal Navy issue money belt. Black shoes to be supplied by ourselves. Instruction on the daily itinerary followed.

A bugle call would sound at six a.m. each weekday and everyone was to parade outside the block at six-fifteen for a morning run. This was followed by an hour to wash and prepare our cabins for inspection. This period was referred to as 'clean ship'. All very nautical. Only after passing an inspection, could the cabin crew head to the canteen for breakfast.

Class room lectures began at nine a.m. sharp, again preceded by a bugle call. Depending on the set timetable, there would be 'boatwork' down on the foreshore or even time set aside for messing about on the river in one of the school's fleet of small craft. To assist in the practicals, we had to obtain a sheath knife with marlin spike.

'Shore leave' (meaning an opportunity to leave the campus) was only permitted at weekends and one evening per week - provided the individual was not rostered for 'guard duty'. This 'duty' seemed unnecessary to anyone rostered. We were not a military establishment but the college principle, Captain Llewellyn, was a Royal Navy reservist and firmly believed in incorporating military discipline into our training.

The duty involved an entire evening or weekend day, spent in the guard room with three other cadets, monitoring the movements of any visitors and keeping records in a log book. At any one time, one of the 'guards' was required to be on the balcony or 'bridge' of the accommodation block and keep a similar log of all the vessels navigating Southampton Water. Binoculars were provided. These stints on the bridge only lasted fifteen minutes before a change of guard, but felt interminable, especially as an icy winter wind was invariably present.

During the initial week, I was measured up for my full blue uniform by a company of merchant navy tailors who attended the school.

The list of clothing items that I had been given to obtain was vast. Everything had to be paid for out of our own pockets and I had to arrange a bank loan to cover the cost. My initial salary was nearly forty pounds a month but my uniform and kit cost three times my monthly income.

If shore leave was granted at a weekend, the cadets taking advantage would parade in full blue uniform before making for the bus taking them into Southampton. Saturday evening would usually be spent in Southampton's Beer Keller before heading to a night club called 'The Bird's Nest'.

Interestingly, wearing full blues had some advantages at that club and frequently the last returning bus to Warsash was missed due to local distractions.

One Sunday morning, following a 'Southampton session' the day before, I was woken by an Iranian cadet who occupied the bunk immediately below my neighbour.

"Nick, look!" he said, pointing to a pile of vomit that had emerged from said neighbour during the night, travelled down the facing wall and across the blanket of the unfortunate as he had turned in his sleep.

The early morning run was a shock to the system and was hated by the cadets. On one run, I was following a cadet through the morning darkness. We were wearing oilskins because of heavy rain when I heard a scream. The cadet in front of me had tripped on a ring bolt by the boat house and I recall seeing the soles of his 'Dunlop Magisters' as he ploughed headlong into the boat pond.

In an attempt to avoid the morning run, I volunteered, with one other cadet to become a bugler.

The bugler escaped due to being on parade in time to rouse everyone else. After making a noise that passed for 'reveille', I got to return to the block in time to wash and get sorted before the runners returned. For several evenings a week, a Royal Marine bugler taught us how to bugle.

My initial training at Warsash lasted three months. In that time, I learned the rudiments of navigation, seamanship, ship construction, meteorology, half-a-dozen associated subjects and, how to make a noise with a bugle.

The next step would involve putting all this valuable knowledge into practice.

I was going to sea.

On Shore Leave March 1973

Chapter 4

Manipur

As I boarded the train at Knebworth railway station en route to Tilbury, I never imagined that I would not return for seven months. The date was Friday, the 20th of April 1972.

The heavy suitcases were a burden, but I stopped off at Tottenham Court Road while passing through London for good reason. Whilst at Warsash, several cadets had obtained a terrific new portable sound system - the cassette player had just made its debut and was considered essential kit. I was able to buy a cheap version as money was tight, but was left with just enough for two cassette tapes. The selection wasn't great but I resumed my journey to Tilbury with Melanie's 'Garden In The City' and Leonard Cohen's 'Songs From A Room' among my luggage.

Seven months - two tapes. Even now, I can recall every note and lyric.

"The ship is called Manipur" I said to the driver of the taxi who drove me into the port complex. We pulled up at a quayside, I climbed out of the taxi and looked up. What a magnificent looking ship, I thought. Huge, freshly painted in a pleasing light grey and white, with the name proudly displayed on the upswept bow. 'Port Chalmers' it read.

"Yours is the one in front" said the taxi driver while struggling with my suitcases.

Tied up along the quayside ahead of Port Chalmers, was a smaller, older tramp ship with rust streaks running vertically down the ship's black hull. Leaning against the bulwarks at the top of the gangway were several figures of asian appearance. The name of this ship, painted on the stern in white and rust was 'Manipur'.

Manipur's black funnel was sporting the blue and white rings of the Brocklebank Line. What was going on? I had signed an agreement with Port line. I had been indoctrinated into the belief that Port Line was the elite of the shipping world. This was evidenced by the magnificent ship tied up immediately behind Manipur. Someone in the personnel department had obviously made a mistake.

"We weren't expecting you until Monday" exclaimed Phillip Ings, the third Officer on board Manipur. "I Don't know where we are going to put you as the ship is in a bit of a mess at the moment" he went on.

So it wasn't a mistake. My first ship was to be this rusty tramp.

Confusion lay in the fact that, at this time, Brocklebank and Port Line were both part of a parent company, Cunard. As such, I was eligible to serve in any ship of Cunard's fleet. From the date of my agreement, it appeared that I was the last ever, Port Line cadet.

By way of consolation, I was able to spend my first night aboard the impressive Port Chalmers. There were no other cadets aboard and I had a double berth cadet cabin to myself.

Next morning I made my way back to the Manipur but there was little activity. Cargo handling had been delayed until the following week which left the weekend free. Apart from the third officer and the Indian crew, the ship seemed deserted. The captain and most other officers had gone ashore for the weekend. I was shown to the pilot's cabin just behind the wheelhouse and told I could make myself at home there until other arrangements were made. The cabin was tiny with just a narrow bunk bed and wash basin. There was no heating and it was cold.

That first weekend aboard Manipur was disappointing. Meals were available in the compact officer's saloon but were very plain, and I learned from the second steward that there were problems with the food stores. The heating was due to be fixed before the ship sailed but in the meantime we would have to make do. On Saturday afternoon, I took the ferry across to Gravesend where I was able to buy a couple of paperbacks. There was very little doing aboard so I spent the remainder of the weekend reading a Sven Hassel novel whilst wrapped in blankets.

On Monday morning, the ship erupted into a hive of activity.

I woke to the sound of heavy steel hatch lids being opened out on the deck. A knock on the cabin door preceded the entry of a figure dressed in working kit. This was Ian Beavis, a cadet who already had sea time. He had a big grin on his face. After introduction, I accompanied Ian out onto the foredeck where cargo was being loaded into the ship's holds. Ian had been instructed by the chief officer, Alistair MacVean, to show me around the workings of Manipur.

The deck was a complex forest of masts, derricks and wire ropes. Stevedores and cargo gangs were at every hatch, stowing the pallets of crates that swung from the quayside and into the ship's cavernous holds. The derricks had been set in 'union purchase' configuration, with electric winches being controlled from small deck houses. Crates were stencilled with their port of destination: Djibouti, Assab and Jeddah amongst others. Place names I had never heard of, but quickly discovered we were bound for the Middle East.

Ian showed me all over Manipur including the bridge and engine room. During frequent tea breaks he enthusiastically told me stories of his own sea adventures.

I learned more about a career at sea during that day than I had in three months at Warsash.

The first job in my chosen career was given to me by our chief officer. It was one of the few tasks that I felt qualified to perform. Standing guard by the spirits locker whilst some very rough-looking dockers placed cases of scotch whiskey, gin and rum inside was, I had been told, of paramount importance. Placing a padlock on the locker door knowing that none of the contents had strayed made me feel like I was earning a proper living at last.

That evening, in the ship's bar, I met the other officers and the few wives that I would be living alongside for the foreseeable future. These strangers all seemed friendly enough, I thought.

On the Tuesday morning I was up early as Manipur was putting to sea. My station was in the wheelhouse with Captain Watkins and Mr Rice, the pilot. I was fascinated by the skills displayed by the crew as the mooring lines were let go in a rehearsed order and tugs assisted manoeuvring Manipur towards the basin exit. Once out in the Thames Estuary, we headed for Chapman's Anchorage where, during the rest of that morning, explosives were loaded into the two forward holds. By lunchtime we were again underway and I spent an hour on the bridge with second officer, John Dobson, before being sent below to catch a late meal.

Once in the dining saloon, I noticed for the first time, a gentle rolling of the ship. I sat at a table opposite Angus McFarlane, the Scottish second steward. I can clearly recall the menu advertising mulligatawny soup which Angus recommended.

"Does the ship usually roll about like this?" I enquired of Angus, just as the soup arrived.

"Aye - now that we've just entered the North Sea you'll notice some movement, but its nae particularly rough - yet".

The meal continued in silence for some time.

Now I don't know whether the confines of that saloon or even the mulligatawny were to blame, but I suddenly felt extremely warm and nauseous.

Before I could finish the soup, I just had time to blurt out "Well I think It's rough!'

I then proceeded to return the entire contents of what I had eaten back into the soup bowl.

My first day at sea would not be forgotten in a hurry.

Chapter 5

Manipur 2

Just my luck. The chief officer entered the dining saloon as I attempted to recover from my close inspection of the soup bowl.

As a result, I spent the rest of the afternoon on a rainswept starboard bridge wing taking in the desolate sights of the North sea. Dressed in yellow oilskins and sou'wester, the driving rain and cold wind met their match. For the first half hour, at least. After that, I could feel the rainwater slowly creeping under the waterproofs and ensuring that the remainder of the watch was less comfortable. Being able to see the motion of the ship as she pitched and rolled, helped deal with my sea-sickness. After an hour or so, I was extremely cold and wet. But the nausea had gone!

I motioned to second officer Dobson through the closed wheelhouse door window that I had recovered and could I please come inside now. He was having none of it and I remained on that exposed bridge wing for the next two hours.

Sea-sickness can have a totally debilitating effect on the sufferer. It can end careers at sea before they have properly begun. I know this because I have met many victims. However, since that afternoon on Manipur's bridge wing, I have never been physically sea sick again.

The 25th of April 1972 found Manipur loading cargo in Rotterdam. Among the cargo were cases of electrical goods manufactured by Philips. Some of the cases had been broken open and part of the contents were missing. I later learned that a small percentage of items to be shipped were normally written off by the insurers as pilferage. Following advice from the chief officer, Ian and I began the forthcoming voyage as proud new owners of Philips electric shavers.

I rather liked Rotterdam, but all too soon we were heading out into The English Channel and steaming for distant ports. Steaming is a misnomer as Manipur was actually a motor vessel with a single, huge, diesel engine. Other terms such as 'sailing' and 'setting sail' really belong to a bygone age as far as modern merchant ships are concerned.

So we 'motored' towards the Middle East. Passage through the Suez Canal would have shortened the voyage considerably but at the time it was closed due to hostilities between Arabs and Israelis. The only alternative was to pass south of The Cape Of Good Hope at the southern tip of Africa and then north towards The Red Sea.

Life on board for a cadet was focused on learning as much about the workings of a ship and its safe navigation as possible. As a result, my time was spent either working with Ian on deck during daylight working hours, or keeping bridge watches with the officer of the watch. These were split into six four-hour periods over a twenty-four hour day. Either twelve to four, four to eight or eight to twelve.

For example, some days would find us chipping and painting a cargo winch or checking lifeboat equipment. If in tropical sunshine, Ian and I would often be stripped down to a pair of denim shorts. On other days, I would be up on the bridge learning how to use a sextant to measure the altitude of the sun for position fixing.

Finding our position in the vastness of the 'oggin' fascinated me from the day we lost sight of land. Watching our navigators calculating position lines from the sun or stars filled me with admiration and cultivated a strong ambition to be as competent as them one day.

Perhaps I would have to stick with this navy lark for a year or two......

When off watch, evenings were often spent socialising in the officer's bar. On a ship like the Manipur, there was little formality and the characters that I shared this small steel island with turned out to be an easy-going bunch. Two wives were among this little group.

Meals on board were regular and more than adequate. As we had an Indian crew, which included the cooks, I was introduced to every variety of authentic curry imaginable. Before joining Manipur, I had never experienced curry. It has since become a lasting association.

To supplement the meals that were provided, we had the opportunity to buy items from the chief steward when he opened his shop or bonded store. These items included cigarettes, spirits, washing requisites and chocolate. They were referred to as 'slops'.

Now I vividly recall being on watch one morning and thinking I would visit the slop store that afternoon to buy some chocolate - a sweet tooth is no friend at sea. When I turned up at the 'slop shop' I was informed by the chief steward that he had none left. In the two weeks we had been at sea, the second engineer's wife had eaten it all. Ample supplies taken on board in Tilbury that should have lasted months, I was told, had all gone! The matter became the subject of frequent discussion in our bar to the embarrassment of the perpetrator. There was no escape on a ship.

At Cape Town, Manipur slowed sufficiently to allow a launch to come alongside. Mail was exchanged along with some important supplies and I was able to send a letter home. Much to my disappointment, there was no chocolate that came aboard and so I promised myself that when I was able, I would put the matter right in grand style.

As it happened, when back in the U.K. six months later, I invaded my local newsagent and spent a small fortune on all the varieties of chocolate that I hadn't seen for so long.

The newsagent was very pleased but I then discovered that I couldn't eat any of it. The taste was not what I remembered - It was horribly, sickly sweet.

That tooth had been lost somewhere in the Indian Ocean.

Chapter 6

Manipur 3

Aden, on the south-west tip of Yemen, was our first port of call. It had now been exactly a month since leaving Europe and we had entered a different world. It was May the 28th, 1972.

We needed fuel oil or 'bunkers' in order to continue to our first discharge port. Manipur dropped anchor and a fuel barge came alongside. This was a job for the engineers, which meant I was able to go ashore by launch just as soon as I had completed the jobs I had been given by the mate.

The heat was blistering and nothing like I had ever experienced. My work was finished in record speed and I wasted no time making for the port.

Big disappointment. Aden was suffering hard times. The town seemed almost deserted and almost all the shops and businesses were closed. This had been a bustling port in its heyday but since British business interests had withdrawn, the economy had collapsed. Only the fuelling of passing ships prevented total dereliction.

Our next ports, Djibouti in Somaliland and Assab on the coast of Ethiopia, were no better. This was the third world and was clearly struggling. No wonder then, that the British Consul in Addis Ababa was desperate for the crates of scotch and gin that we had brought.

I was determined to see as much of these ports as time permitted but was never reluctant to return to the Manipur. At about this time, the ship's air-conditioning began to regularly fail which created almost unbearable temperatures in the accommodation. I took to wearing only shorts and sandals for most of the day.

After a short stop at Hodeidah on the Saudi coast, Manipur left for Aqaba. Scuttles were fitted to open port holes to catch the slightest breeze and direct it into our cabin spaces. The sea surface was like glass and the sun fierce. My white body was turning lobster and I started to cover up whenever outside. Often, dolphins or porpoises would race alongside the ship for nautical miles.

Aqaba was our discharge port for the explosives we were carrying. Tons of tank shells were loaded on to Jordanian military trucks for their British-built tanks. Jordan, being an Arab nation, was preparing for any future conflict with their Israeli neighbours. Chief officer MacVean confided in me that on a recent previous trip, Manipur had delivered a similar cargo to the Israelis just a short distance away in Eilat. Armaments were big earners in this part of the world and the U.K. was not missing out.

The chief officer had a job for me while in port. He wanted me to act as a chaperone to the two wives we had aboard so that they could visit the ancient lost city of Petra. Would I go? I was changed and ready to leave before he had finished telling me about it.

One hundred kilometres north-north-east of Aqaba, an extra wonder of the world is located. The taxi journey to Petra took nearly four hours across empty, arid desert. The road surface was poor and there was very little traffic. This was real Lawrence of Arabia country. Fortunately, the taxi driver found the lost city without great difficulty, leaving us plenty of time to explore. Although a tourist attraction today, back in 1972, Petra had very few visitors and this fact contributed to its mystique. To this day it remains one of the most impressive destinations I have visited.

From Aqaba, Manipur plied her trade along the Red Sea coast by delivering the remainder of our European cargo in Port Sudan and Jeddah. Then we returned to Aqaba to load phosphates for India. Eleven thousand tons of it. After refuelling again in Aden we set off for India, arriving in Madras around the 10th of July.

Crossing the two thousand, five hundred miles of Indian Ocean had been an adventure in itself. Manipur was sick. In addition to an air-conditioning system that had given up even pretending to work, we had a main engine failure. For several days the ship was adrift without any power. Fresh water was in short supply and the sun was intense.

Showers were at first rationed and later banned. Washing, of any kind was limited, and everyone on board was constantly covered in perspiration. We did have a fridge in the bar that worked, but any cans placed in it never got chance to cool.

However, being adrift provided an opportunity for shark fishing. I watched from the bridge wing as crew members tried their luck. The third mate tied some meat to a piece of wire and before long, Manipur was surrounded by sharks of all sizes. A huge specimen was finally landed on deck and only approached after considerable time had elapsed. The brave soul doing the approaching, whilst armed with a heavy rail stancheon, was rewarded by being chased along the deck by the demented 'nobby'. He narrowly escaped losing a limb by diving into a deck housing.

Madras was followed by a longer stay in Calcutta. The heat was oppressive and many of our crew had suffered one ailment or another due to the conditions. The air-con had to be repaired. As a result, all non-essential officers and the two wives were accommodated at the Marine Club near the dock. Happily, I was considered non-essential enough to spend an entire weekend at this club. There was a large swimming pool, snooker rooms and a vast bar area where gin and fresh lime was a house speciality. For those two days, I felt like royalty.

When the Manipur was habitable again, I was back aboard assisting with the discharge of our cargo of phosphate. The work was dirty and the hours were long but I still made use of any spare time to go ashore.

On one such occasion, I was returning to the ship along with Ian. Rickshaw drivers were hounding us for business, so we obliged by taking a seat in two of the available vehicles. The drivers were actually pullers as there was no motor - power being supplied by the puller's legs. One rupee was the tariff but as we set off, I noticed Ian bribing his man to run ahead. A race began when I offered my 'driver' three rupees if we reached our ship first. Both rickshaws were hurtling towards the port and about neck and neck when I heard a blood-curdling scream. My 'driver' suddenly flung his arms in the air and disappeared between the wheels of his own cart. The rickshaw's handles lurched alarmingly upwards before settling and it became apparent that I had lost.

The poor man had tripped and suffered gravel rash so I ensured he took home a generous second prize that day. I was later told that these rickshaw 'pilots' had a disturbingly short life span.

From Calcutta, Manipur headed for Chalna in Bangladesh to load Jute. This was little more than a jungle clearing alongside a navigable river. Here I witnessed extreme poverty among the population, but at least we were helping to build their economy. I was quite glad to leave.

On August the 14th, Manipur arrived in Colombo, Ceylon (Now Sri Lanka) to load tea for the Americans. Ceylon was a like a breath of fresh air. Colombo bustled and no opportunity was missed to explore.

Loading our cargo was slow and with engine repairs needed, there would be ample time to see beyond the port. In fact, being a cadet, coupled with having wives on board, was a perfect recipe for exploration. These wives had heard about tours into the island's interior - and of course they needed a chaperone. I had landed. On a road trip to the town of Kandy in the heartland, our taxi stopped at Elephant's Pass. Grabbing hold of the wiry hairs of an elephant's head, I headed off on a mini safari. For some reason, the animal had a twitch causing it's right ear to smack against my right thigh several times. This was the asian variety that was supposed to have the smaller ears.

The resulting bruise remained with me for weeks. No matter, we were now heading for the U.S.A.!

Chapter 7

Manipur 4

Before leaving Colombo, a third cadet joined us. Nick Senanayeke was Celanese, and the son of Ceylon's Minister for Education.

Re-crossing the Indian Ocean for bunkers in Durban, was a totally different experience to our shark-fishing days in placid, deep blue water. The air-conditioning had been repaired but was not now needed. The southern hemisphere was in mid winter. High winds had whipped up the sea to a heavy swell and Manipur struggled to maintain her sixteen knots. The temperature dropped as we slowly made our way south-west, and cold weather kit became necessary.

No opportunity to go ashore in Durban as the bunkers were taken aboard with South African efficiency. Just time to post a few letters and then we were away again.

The sea was particularly rough rounding the southern coast of Africa. Currents in this part of the world are notoriously unpredictable and dozens of shipwrecks litter the seabed. Each cadet was now engaged on a bridge watch with one of the watch keeping officers. This was an opportunity to learn and practice maritime navigation using charts, compass, sextant and chronometer in the traditional manner. Satellite navigation was for the future.

Our passage from Durban to the east coast of the U.S.A. took three weeks. During the voyage across the South Atlantic and then into the North Atlantic, the weather changed dramatically. Heavy sweaters and barathea trousers were exchanged for thin white shirts and shorts as we passed through The Doldrums. Here, there was barely a breath of wind for a whole week. This was the part of the globe where sailing ships would often be becalmed. Manipur however, ploughed through the flat-calm sea at her steady sixteen knots with only the odd Albatross for company. At least the main engine was now behaving itself since a piston had been exchanged.

Manipur arrived in Wilmington, North Carolina, on the 19th of September 1972. Between deck watches to assist in the part-discharge of tea and hessian, every opportunity was taken to go ashore. Nick, the Celanese cadet, insisted we visit the first hamburger restaurant we could find as he had described such venues in great detail prior to our arrival on the coast. That first American hamburger was a revelation. Twice as big as a British Wimpy and included all sorts of salad and sauce. My friendship with dill pickle and onions originated right there.

From Wilmington, our ship visited other ports in the southern states. These included Savannah, Port Everglades, Mobile, New Orleans, Galveston and Houston.

On our approach to The Houston Ship Canal, I was summoned to the bridge by Captain Watkins to take the ship's wheel. As part of a cadet's training, experience in ship steering and handling is necessary. A steering certificate was a requirement of the Board of Trade.

All very exciting for an eighteen-year old who hadn't yet learned to drive a car. Rather nerve-wracking too. This could have been done in the open sea, but Manipur used auto-pilot when crossing oceans. Now we were in a narrow, dredged channel that needed precise alterations of course to prevent grounding.

Our American pilot came aboard, had a short conversation with our captain and noticed me standing behind the ship's wheel, clutching it as if my life depended on it.

In a broad texan accent he commented "Your crew sure look mighty young, cap'n".

He was right. When I was eighteen, I only looked about twelve.

Manipur edged into the canal at slow speed. "How fast can she go cap'n?" enquired the pilot.

Captain Watkins removed the ubiquitous pipe from his mouth and proudly replied "Oh, she'll do a good sixteen knots if we need it".

At that, the pilot turned his cap so that the peak was facing backwards, grabbed hold of the wheelhouse rail, and mockingly exclaimed " Okay cap'n - let her rip!"

Manipur's telegraph was altered to half ahead and I was given instructions to keep her steady.

Not as easy as it may sound. A nine-thousand-ton, five-hundred-foot long ship needs time to respond to any turns on the wheel. If the bow veered off to either port or starboard, then only a very gentle movement was needed to bring her back on course. Too much, and the ship would over steer with embarrassing consequences. A narrow seaway such as this was not an ideal practice ground. My concentration was later broken by the pilot trying to communicate by radio telephone with the crew of a huge barge that had emerged from a bend in the canal. There was no response to his increasingly anxious calls.

"Hell, I don't like this one bit!" he exclaimed to Captain Watkins. The pilot then turned to me:

"Hard-a-starboard, son! Full astern, cap'n!"

What! Did he really mean that? Captain Watkins looked at me and nodded. I spun the wheel clockwise and waited. Ever-so-slowly, Manipur's bow turned to the right. We began to head straight for the nearside bank of the canal.

The terrifying thought crossed my mind: Had I made a mistake? Starboard was to the right, wasn't it? I had heard him correctly hadn't I? Too late now - the ship's bow crashed through a wooden jetty protruding from the nearest land. Huge pieces of timber flew into the air and came crashing down on to the foredeck. Then Manipur's bow lurched upwards as we hit the shore. The entire ship shuddered to a grinding halt and I felt numb. I was waiting for total condemnation.

"Well done, son!" the pilot calmly remarked. Captain Watkins looked as dumbfounded as I felt.

"Do you think we might have sunk that barge if we hadn't taken evasive action?" the captain asked the pilot.

"Sunk it? That was a liquid-petroleum-gas carrier we just avoided. If we had hit that thing, it would probably have exploded. It would have taken us with it - and most of Houston, too"

It took several attempts to free Manipur from its temporary berth, but by running the engine at full astern, the ship gradually came free from the embankment. The chief officer was on the fo'c's'le and reported only slight damage to the ship's stem.

What a day! We berthed that afternoon without further incident and I was able to retire to the bar.

That night, I went to my bunk with the comforting thought that I had saved Manipur, and all who sailed in her, from certain death. Not to mention the local population.

My steering certificate was duly endorsed by Captain Watkins.

Chapter 8

From Tramp To A Lady

Leaving the Southern States of America bound for Europe on the 28th of October 1972, was met with mixed feelings. Yes, the thought of home leave was welcome, but the memories of all that I had experienced in last six months couldn't be matched at home.

Crossing the North Atlantic with winter approaching, was another passage that would test anyone's ability to mentally and physically resist sea-sickness. I was now fully used to the Manipur's rolling and pitching and even considered crashing through a heavy sea to be quite thrilling.

One thought however, always troubled me. What if disaster struck and all souls had to take to the open lifeboats? In company with Ian and Nick, we had done our best to ensure that both boats were well-maintained, equipped, and provisioned - but even so, I wouldn't fancy our chances if ever we had to take to the lifeboats in the kind of weather we encountered.

Sleeping while wearing a life-jacket, I discovered, was too uncomfortable so the practice was soon abandoned. Just the same, the jacket became a friend that often followed me around the ship in stormy weather.

'Board of Trade sports', or more correctly, muster drill, was held every week - weather permitting.

An alarm, or seven short blasts on the ship's whistle, would trigger the assembling of all crew that were not watch-keeping at their lifeboat station. Usually the boats would be partly lowered to check the gravity davits hadn't seized, and fire hoses rolled out to be pointed at a pretend fire.

Weather conditions didn't permit any such drill on this particular crossing, and Manipur arrived at the Weser River estuary in northern Germany intact.

I met the German pilot at the head of the Jacob's ladder that had been lowered to the pilot boat.

He spoke perfect English and seemed jovial. I escorted him to the wheelhouse where the captain and third officer were waiting.

"Good morning captain, and welcome to Germany" The pilot said as he held out his hand to Captain Watkins.

Captain Watkins's response was simply a reluctant grunt. He then turned his back on the German and stared ahead at the river mouth.

I later learned that Captain Watkins hated Germans. In 1940, on his first trip to sea, Cadet Watkins's ship had the misfortune to be torpedoed and sunk. Our captain survived, but became a prisoner of the German Navy. Many of his shipmates had been killed when his ship was destroyed, and Cadet Watkins spent the remainder of the war in a German prisoner-of-war camp.

If only I had known earlier, I could have plagued him for stories of his wartime exploits during the many visits he made to the wheelhouse when at sea. Captain Watkins was highly regarded by all his officers, but was a reclusive character for reasons best known to himself.

Sadly, in many respects, Bremerhaven was our penultimate port. Tilbury was only a day's passage away and that was where I left the tramping Manipur, never to meet again.

I had been at sea for almost seven months and covered thirty-eight thousand miles. I had visited ten different countries on four continents.

But now It was the 16th of November 1972, and I was going home on leave.

Contracted officers earned leave according to the length of time spent away. For cadets, leave was calculated on the basis that they could be be required to join any of the company's ships, anywhere, at a moments notice.

As it happened, I wasn't required again until the New Year. I had almost seven weeks to spend with family and friends. To have Christmas at home was a bonus and wasn't wasted. I travelled to London frequently to replace and obtain new kit and clothing. I gained a better cassette player and a decent collection of tapes. My two originals were worn out.

My leave ended on the third of January, 1973. On the following morning, I said my farewells and took the train to Southampton where I was fortunate enough to meet a real lady.

Standing on the quayside and looking up at Port Caroline, I experienced vivid memories of comparing Manipur with Port Chalmers in Tilbury the previous spring. The Caroline and Chalmers were sisters, the newest and most magnificent ships ever to fly the Port Line house flag.

Once aboard, I met with other cadets - two deck, and one engineer. My accommodation was to be a double cabin which I was to share with a first-tripper who introduced himself as 'Trigger'.

The other deck cadet had fulfilled his sea time to qualify for a second mate's certificate, but had recently failed his exam. Nonetheless, he had persuaded the personnel department to allow him to wear fourth mate's insignia on his uniform and his ego was increased accordingly.

Port Caroline was complemented by a British crew and there was further accommodation for twelve passengers. Unlike Manipur, this ship appeared spotless, but standards all round were higher and that included personal appearance. Uniform was to be worn at all times when aboard and if dining with passengers, then mess kit, including cummerbunds were to be worn.

Deck cadets were expected to comply with a strict Port Line working routine. At seven a.m. each day, it was necessary to report to the chief officer who would give instructions for that day's duties. In port, this would usually involve cargo working or deck maintenance with the crew. At sea, there were opportunities for watch keeping on the bridge or further deck maintenance. Breakfast would have to wait until eight a.m. or later.

Fully laden, the Caroline slipped her moorings and entered Southampton Water during that first week in January. I was on the bridge when, on our port side, we glided past The School Of Navigation at Warsash. No doubt some 'sprog' was noting our passage in the school's log.

Out into The Solent and altering course to starboard, we headed for the English Channel. Soon we would be 'deep sea', bound for the Panama Canal and New Zealand.

North Atlantic, 1973

Chapter 9

South Pacific

P ort Caroline crossed the North Atlantic Ocean on a south westerly course heading for Panama.

As usual, in the winter months, the Atlantic was living up to its reputation. I was determined to capture the ferocity of the sea during this passage on film. Secured by rope, I ventured on deck briefly with my 'Mickey Mouse' Kodak 110 cassette camera, which had been a Christmas present.

I only had black and white film in the camera, but captured some images which I still have.

I didn't hang about - waves were slamming into the side of the ship and breaking above my head.

Into The Caribbean and the sea moderated. By the time we anchored off Cristobal at the Atlantic end of the canal, Port Caroline had become a familiar home, and despite the discipline, I enjoyed the routine. The fourth mate was a pain at times but all the other officers were pleasant enough.

With the sea behaving itself, and a clear horizon visible, I was able to take a 'sun sight' using a sextant and calculate a position line for the first time. I had learned how to take such sights on the Manipur but never practiced the complex calculations required for position fixing.

As we were carrying passengers, one of my responsibilities included keeping them informed of our progress. A large, formica map of the world was fixed inside the passenger accommodation access door. Each day at noon, I would mark the ship's position on the map, along with the distance travelled over the previous twenty-four hours.

Meals on board were taken in the officer's saloon and our passengers were included. The seating arrangements ensured I was regularly interrogated by the passengers allocated to my table. Silver table service was the order of the day, and meals were prepared to a high standard. I certainly had no complaints, although I missed the Manipur's special curries.

I wrote a letter home while at anchor which I discovered forty two years later among my dad's correspondence. I never knew that he had kept some of the letters I had written whilst at sea.

Transiting The Panama Canal was another exciting experience. For most of the eight hour passage I was on the bridge. My pocket camera at hand. I had one cassette of colour film so I had to use the Kodak sparingly.

Out into The Pacific Ocean and the beginning of ten days of relatively calm blue ocean and continuous sunshine. Port Caroline was capable of twenty one knots, which averaged out at about five hundred nautical miles per day. We would be gliding through five thousand miles of vast South Pacific Ocean before reaching our destination at the southern tip of New Zealand.

There really was nothing much to see - except sea. There were plenty of dolphins and an albatross which followed us for two days, but no land. I caught sight of one ship travelling in the opposite direction. It was our sister ship, Port Chalmers. So I had to take a photograph.

The cadets on board were supplemented by two other lads who were working their passage to New Zealand. Their fathers were both senior personnel within the shipping company. Between us, we must have painted every bollard and winch aboard before reaching land.

On the 28th of January 1973, having reached longitude 94 degrees, 5 minutes west, we crossed the equator. Preparations had been made for a ceremony in which anyone 'crossing the line' for the first time would be subject to an ordeal by 'Neptune's assistants'.

There was no point in my remonstrating that I had crossed the line twice before on the Manipur.

I was one of those hauled before Neptune on the afterdeck. After interrogation, crew members carrying buckets covered me from head to toe in an evil mix of 'gunge', I was then knocked about by some large wet fish and finally carried and thrown into our swimming pool. I was now numbered as one of Neptune's trusty shellbacks. I even have the certificate to prove it.

The sky at night fascinated me. In the vastness of the Pacific there is no ambient light to hinder the light from stars and planets. I had a book with me written by Patrick Moore and used it to discover the names of the principle stars, planets and constellations.

Bridge watches at night frequently generated conversation about the night sky. I can vividly recall standing on the bridge wing in a warm breeze, with only the sound made by the race of sea water along the ship's side, and 'thrum' of the engines. Looking at the sky through binoculars, it was possible to see more clearly at sea than from land. 'Shooting stars' became a common sight.

The second mate described our first port of call as 'not just bad, but extra bad'. He was referring to Bluff, a small settlement on the southern extremity of New Zealand. Its very existence was due to the export of lamb and mutton. This was sheep farming country.

As soon as Port Caroline had berthed, meat loaders were swung over the ship's holds and the loading process began. At my first opportunity to go ashore, I went for a long walk to the top of the bluff that gave the port its name. Looking southwards, there was nothing but open sea. The nearest land would be Antarctica.

I took some photographs and returned to the port. The second mate had been right, there was nothing in the tiny township to interest visitors. Apart from a cluster of wooden houses, the only building of note was a small cafe that advertised itself as a 'milk bar'.

On entering this attraction, I met with some of the crew who heartily endorsed the milk shakes on offer. These were bottled, so I asked for banana flavour.

"We only sell vanilla" said the young woman who put a bottle of what appeared to be plain milk on the counter.

"That'll be twenty cents".

I thought that was very reasonable, and handed her a dollar note.

She gave me the change and added "When you return the bottle, you'll get ten cents back".

Alongside At Bluff

Chapter 10

South Pacific 2

Port Caroline's next port of call was Timaru on the east coast of south island, New Zealand.

Here, the 'wharfies' started work early and finished early so there was time to explore the town in the late afternoon and evenings. I discovered a small music shop that had a few guitars on display and ventured inside. The salesman I encountered convinced me I could easily learn to play without tuition and I left his shop with a second-hand Yamaha guitar and a Simon and Garfunkel song book. On our return voyage, I practised playing in the cadet's study without much success and eventually sold the guitar to a friend during my next leave. I wouldn't pick up another until forty years later.

Our last loading port in New Zealand was Maunganui on the east coast of north island. I took a long hike to the top of Mount Maunganui to take photographs which now reside in one of my albums. Moored behind the Caroline was a diminutive naval frigate. By invitation, I attended a cocktail party aboard this frigate with other Caroline officers and was amazed to learn that they had a complement of two hundred and sixty all ranks. By comparison, the Caroline was four times as big with a total complement of fifty.

From Maunganui it was a straight run back to Panama with a full cargo of frozen meat, butter and cheese. This was enough to supply the whole of the U.K. for a week.

The only land we saw during the passage was 'Rapa Iti', a volcanic island that rises from the seabed. It is one of the remotest, inhabited islands on Earth.

Some five hundred miles west of the Galapagos Islands, our third mate spotted a distress flare on our port side during the forenoon watch. The captain was summoned and the ship altered course towards the source. I was on the after deck at the time, having been given a painting job, but as soon as Caroline began to swing to port, I went to the rail to investigate. Something was up, a ship of our size would not need to alter course so dramatically in an ocean as vast as the Pacific if there wasn't good reason.

I couldn't see anything from the deck, so I went to the wheelhouse where there was considerable activity. From the bridge wing I saw a small sailing boat that appeared very low in the water. Two figures were waving franticly, and as we came alongside, a rope ladder was lowered. The two figures turned out to be a Malcolm and Merrill Robson from Sark, in the Channel Islands.

These two adventurers had set out some months before and were attempting to sail around the world. Their tiny yacht, The Maid Of Malham, had sprung a serious leak and they were slowly sinking. For two days they had been baling water and were close to exhaustion. Amazingly, they didn't even have a working radio, so if they hadn't been spotted, they would very soon have gone down with their boat.

Needless to say, they were extremely grateful to have been rescued, and despite the chief engineer offering to salvage their craft, they were happy to leave it to sink. I have in my photo album the last photograph ever taken of The Maid Of Malham.

The Robsons wrote a poem about their rescue which was copied, signed, and given to the officers. My copy still lives in a scrapbook that I compiled.

As a cadet in training, I had a workbook and a journal that was supplied by the company and was inspected at frequent intervals. Whenever a particular task was completed satisfactorily three times, it would be signed off by the chief officer and used as evidence of progress. I kept both books until my agreement with the company had been fulfilled but had to surrender them on completion. Pity - they would have been an interesting record for future reference.

Another transit of the fascinating Panama Canal and into the Caribbean. I was now keeping bridge watches with the third mate and practised laying courses through the island groups.

The North Atlantic was better behaved on our return crossing than it was when outward bound. Also, as the Caroline was fully laden, she was more stable now. The voyage out to New Zealand had been in 'ballast' - a term used to describe an empty ship save for ballast water in the double-bottom tanks. As a result, the ship was tossed around as if made of balsa wood.

On the 30th of March 1973, Port Caroline berthed at Avonmouth, near Bristol, and the discharge of our cargo began. As I had only been aboard for three months I wasn't expecting leave, but the news that I was going home was met with jubilation. I never met a seafarer who didn't value leave.

I caught a train from Bristol to London in the early afternoon and was home that evening. Three months at sea would usually equate to three weeks leave for a cadet at that time. However, after less than two weeks at home, the telephone rang. It was Mike Taylor from Fleet Personnel.

"Sorry to cut your leave short, but we'd like you to be ready to join your next ship in Southampton tomorrow. I realise it is rather short notice, but will you able to do that for me?" Mike said.

Plans I had conceived for the following week would have to be scrapped. I was not really in a position to refuse.

"What ship are you wanting me to join, Mike?" was all I could manage.

"Well, I think you might like this one - it's the Queen Elizabeth Two".

Chapter 11

From A Lady To A Queen

Southampton on a fine Spring morning. It was 12th April 1973.
The railway journey from home had been uneventful but the two heavy Globe-Trotter suitcases were slowing me down as I entered the Cunard building in Canute Road.

Hours later I was standing on the Quayside of Ocean Terminal looking up at my new home.

What an impressive sight! Queen Elizabeth 2 towered above the terminal buildings and all along the quayside there was great activity.

A uniformed security guard scrutinised the pass that had taken so long to be issued that morning and I was shown access via a starboard embarkation door where I was at last relieved of my suitcases. Numerous security staff were on hand checking identity documents and I watched as my luggage disappeared into a short tunnel before emerging ahead.

I had never witnessed a luggage x-ray machine before.

Next, a deck plan was handed to me and told my cabin number was S1 which I would find way up on the sports deck on the starboard side.

Fast forward the next forty minutes or so while I endeavoured to locate S1 by asking crew members who seemed equally confused. The suitcases became physically heavier.

Eventually a member of cruise staff came to my aid and within a few minutes I was standing inside my quarters for the next four months.

It was a double berth with bunk beds, two desks, two chairs, two wardrobes, in fact, two of every thing but only one of me. Was I going to share?

I began unpacking but soon there was a knock on the door.

"Are you Cadet Eliason?" said the uniformed stranger. I confirmed that I was.

"Good. You are wanted on the bridge. If you change into full blues quickly I will take you up there.

You will need all your identity documents as security is very tight".

Fifteen minutes later I was in front of a thick steel door and being asked for my security pass.

Rather odd that the request should come from a man dressed in casual clothing.

The door was opened for me and I walked for the first time into the wheelhouse of QE2.

It was smaller than I had imagined. In fact not much bigger than the wheelhouse of the Port Caroline that I had left less than two weeks previously. The ship's wheel was tiny at about twelve inches diameter. What impressed me the most was the plethora of individual controls and electrical systems.

While taking this in, a large uniformed figure that had been over by the wheelhouse door, turned towards me. This was First Officer

Robin Woodall. He told me that my job for the next four hours was to monitor the telephones and report to him any developments while he was attending to work in the chartroom which was located just behind the wheelhouse. He then left.

So there I was, alone and to all intents and purposes at just nineteen years old, in charge of the most prestigious passenger ship in the world!

Now I knew that keeping a bridge watch whilst in port and safely secured to the quayside was a bit of a nonsense. All those months spent on Manipur and Port Caroline confirmed that there was a big difference between what was necessary and what was not. Besides, who was likely to call up to the bridge when we weren't even going anywhere?

I began to study all the switches, controls and lights while waiting for that elusive telephone call, when my attention was drawn to a movement on the quayside. A crane with a rope net containing wooden crates was being hoisted and swung towards the starboard bridge wing. The net was then lowered onto the teak planking and a figure appeared from a small hatchway in the structure behind.

Odd. Passenger ships wouldn't be taking cargo on the bridge wing, and considering I had been left in charge of the most important part of the ship I immediately opened the wing door to investigate.

The small man I had seen was now climbing back through the hatchway having released the rope net from the crane. I approached the hatchway and took a look inside. Not what I expected at all.

I saw several men removing Sterling sub-machine guns from already opened crates and stowing them in overhead racks.

While gawping, the face that belonged to the figure I had seen previously appeared just inches from mine and obstructed my view.

"Do you need something?" said the man.

A little lost for words, I uttered something along the lines "Just curious - I'm in charge of the bridge you know!"

"And I'm in charge of something that needs to be kept secret. So I suggest you p**s off and let me get on with it."

Cheek! I turned and went directly to where I found First Officer Woodall poring over a chart. Having told him what had happened, he straightened, threw down the pencil he had been holding and stormed off in the direction I had just come.

I heard raised voices but moments later the officer returned.

"What did he say sir?"

First Officer Woodall looked at me. I could see his face was quite red.

"He told me to p**s off as well!"

Postscript:

Keeping secrets I can do, but it would have been helpful to know beforehand that members of the Special Air Service and Royal Marines were going to be with us for a while.

I knew nothing of the adventure about to begin until QE2 was out in The English Channel and bound for Israel. Only then, at a convivial meeting in the Staff Captain's cabin did I learn that our magnificent liner - the pride of the British Merchant Navy - had been threatened with destruction.

Chapter 12

Israel Saga

How exciting! At any moment we could be subject to terrorist attack.

Having left the Straits of Gibraltar in our wake, we were steaming eastwards.

QE2 was cutting through the Mediterranean at full speed. I was allocated bridge watches with two other officers and working four-hour patterns.

At the beginning of each watch I had to pass through a checkpoint of thinly disguised but armed Royal Marine Commandos. Access to the bridge was via a locked steel door that could only be opened from the inside. Steel gratings had been fitted over the bridge wing companionways and we could take comfort from the fact that, as a last resort, we had a double-barrelled 12 bore shotgun and a box of cartridges in the wheelhouse.

How British! No terrorist group armed with AK 47 assault rifles and grenades would have stood a chance against a determined deck officer with a shotgun. Provided of course that the terrorist group allowed time for said deck officer to fumble with the box of cartridges and figure out how to load the thing. Naturally, no training was given.

From the island of Crete to the port of Ashdod on the coast of Israel, I was given instructions to monitor one of our radar sets and pay particular attention to any fast moving echoes.

Of course no one on board knew what form the threat may take.

It transpired later that Muammar Gadafi of Libya had arranged for two ex-Soviet submarines to attack QE2 with torpedoes with the aim of sending her to become the latest addition to Davy Jones's locker.

However, I'm pleased that he failed.

QE2 arrived safely in Ashdod under escort, courtesy of the Israeli Navy. The Israeli military were everywhere. Divers began checking the underwater hull for mines and soldiers lined the quayside. I was particularly impressed to see that many were female and all armed with the ubiquitous Uzi sub-machine gun.

We could now retire the 12 bore.

Bridge watches were retained but because the hours were extended with corresponding free time, I had plenty of opportunities to take advantage of shore visits and excursions.

During our stay in Haifa it was decided by Relief Staff Captain Ridley that the forward observation deck could use a fresh coat of paint. The few passengers who had braved the outward voyage had mostly left to celebrate the twenty-fifth anniversary of the founding of the State of Israel.

The tiny numbers on board were unlikely to miss the use of the observation deck in the time taken to paint it.

This job was allocated to Cadet Eliason. After all, having completed two previous voyages on cargo ships he would be well qualified in the art of painting.

So, in accordance with common sense, I roped off the access companionways to the observation deck and obtained a twenty-five litre can of deck green paint with roller.

The day was fine and sunny. Quite a pleasant job really. Within short time I had covered a large area with the thick green paint.

Then WHOOSHHH!!

An Israeli air force jet flew fast and low over QE2. Followed by another, then another.

Now I didn't know that Captain Ridley was entertaining guests in his cabin. Or that he had a door that opened onto the observation deck. Or that there would be a fly past that would attract so much attention. In the event, I must have been responsible for altering the colour of at least four pairs of shoes. Probably more.

I could tell he wasn't happy and after a brief exchange with Officer Hutcheson, I offered to rope his door closed. I was advised in certain unrepeatable terms, that that wouldn't be necessary as the damage had already been done.

There were no apologies for my spoiled paintwork.

I made good the spoiled surface with an extra-thick layer of paint In the meantime, Captain Ridley's guests had been replaced by others.

Then WHOOSHHH!!

The Air Force was back. I remember hearing a stifled shout. Too late. That same door flew open and I claimed my next victims.

Postscript:

In Dubai today where QE2 resides, there may be, under countless layers of paint, a series of shoe prints created in 1973 which have become a part of forgotten QE2 history.

On QE2 Bridge Wing, 1973

Chapter 13

Cruising In Style

On berthing at Ocean Terminal in Southampton after the failed terrorist attempt to sink QE2, I was tasked with ensuring the Royal Marines and S.A.S were discretely landed at Marchwood. That night, a launch was lowered for embarkation on the port side, out of sight from the terminal. With two of QE2's crew, I transported the soldiers, who were in civilian clothes, across Southampton Water to their collection point. I had been advised not to mention the role played by these men as their presence on board during the Israel venture was supposed to be a secret. What we didn't know at that time was the fact that the press had already exposed the operation, and amusing cartoons had already appeared in the national newspapers.

Into the summer season and QE2 began her cruising itinerary. This magnificent ship had been built for a dual purpose. She was the last liner ever designed to cope with the rigours encountered on regular North Atlantic crossings between Southampton and New York. She was equally suited to cruising. Just as well, since air travel was taking an ever greater share of the Atlantic trade.

Cruising with a full complement of passengers was a pleasant experience. In early June 1973, having called at Lisbon, QE2 passed through the Gibraltar Strait on a ten day tour of Mediterranean ports. Someone among the passenger list must have had very strong connections since a rendezvous with the American aircraft carrier, John F Kennedy, had been arranged. I was fortunate to be on the bridge of QE2 when the carrier approached and maintained a parallel course on our starboard side.

A Sea King helicopter transferred Admiral Pringle, the commander of the American sixth fleet, along with some of his naval officers, to our foredeck. He was escorted to our bridge and introduced to Captain Law and those of us present. He made a remark about my youthful appearance and suggested I might make captain of QE2 before I was thirty. I was surprised by the remark but didn't disagree.

Phantom, and other jet aircraft were launched from the carrier to provide a spectacular, but loud air display. The top brass from both ships gathered on the starboard bridge wing to watch as the jets turned and flew directly overhead. Although stationed in the wheelhouse, I took the opportunity to join the group out on the bridge wing and handed my camera to our coxswain for a photograph. Passengers crowded the observation deck to secure a view of the display. One of the aircraft approached unseen from QE2's stern at such a low level that these passengers were taken completely by surprise. The majority ducked and scattered in all directions.

The rendezvous with the aircraft carrier was one of the highlights of the Mediterranean cruise which included visits to ports in Greece and Italy.

Our next cruise was to Norway. I had been on duty for a long period during our crossing of the North Sea but was able to get some sleep before our arrival. My first recollection was waking up to the sound of music being played through the ship's address system. The piece being played was 'Morning' by Edvard Grieg, the Norwegian composer. I looked out through my cabin window and saw a vertical rock face on our starboard side not more than a quarter mile away. I dressed and went out onto the boat deck. The rock face towered above the ship and was lost in low cloud.

From the observation deck, it seemed as if we were passing along a tunnel due to another rock face on the port side at a similar distance. I found the Norwegian fjords fascinating.

At the North Cape, our launches were lowered to the water and were used to transfer passengers to the shore for the trek of a lifetime. The passengers who took advantage had to walk miles to watch the sun pass close to the horizon and rise again without setting. We were now in the land of the midnight sun. I enjoyed being captain of my own launch even if it meant not joining the trek. When the time came to collect the adventurers, I could see disappointment on their faces. On that particular afternoon the sky was overcast and the sun hidden from view.

At Hammerfest, QE2 dropped anchor some distance from the port as there were insufficient berthing facilities. The entire length of anchor cable was used since the water in this, and most fjords we visited, could be incredibly deep.

Our diesel engined motor launches were again used to ferry passengers from the ship to shore.

Fourteen was the number on the launch I was given command of. Steve Lockey, an engineer cadet, was my chief engineer. Running the launch at top speed to transfer as many passengers as possible was exciting, but must have created undue stress on the engine. On our third or fourth run to the quayside, I put the lever control to full astern to take headway off the craft and bring the fully laden launch to a perfect halt alongside the quay. Nothing happened. The engine wouldn't reverse and all I could do was stop the motor completely and throw our mooring lines to the crewmen on the quay. Fortunately, the promenade ahead was raised on concrete pillars and I was able to steer between them and give our passengers an unrestricted view of its underside.

On our return journey later that day, having sorted the engine sufficiently to be able to select reverse, another problem surfaced.

A tap on the shoulder from Steve brought my attention to the launch's rear cabin which was packed with passengers. Thick grey smoke was now billowing from the engine casing and filling the cabin with acrid fumes. Through the smoke I could see many pairs of worried-looking eyes. I stopped the engine and with help from volunteers, managed to clear most of the smoke. Number fourteen limped back to QE2 and was not used again that day. To my surprise, I was thanked by the disembarking passengers and nobody complained. The red ensign flag from this troublesome launch now resides in my office at home.

Between cruises, QE2 made Atlantic crossings from Southampton to New York. On one of these, the sea was so rough and the swell so heavy, that even the ship's stabilisers were overwhelmed.

I was present in the wheelhouse with an anxious-looking Captain Law, when the bow of the ship plunged into a sea and was completely submerged for several worrying seconds. As the bow slowly lifted, a huge wave slammed into the forward superstructure and rose as far as the bridge.

For another few seconds, cascading water was all that could be seen from the wheelhouse windows. When relieved, I took a rather staggered walk around the public rooms. Very few passengers had ventured from their cabins and the restaurants were deserted. In the cabin corridors, stewards had placed sickness bags at frequent intervals, but even with such precautions, I saw small piles of sawdust in an attempt to soak up evidence of sea sickness.

During Atlantic crossings, one of my principle responsibilities was the plotting of icebergs on a chart specifically set aside for the purpose. Sightings of icebergs from other sources were received via a fax machine and transferred to the chart. By constantly laying off the QE2's position from our satellite navigation system, warning of the presence of icebergs in our vicinity could be given. I was determined the ship would not suffer the fate of the Titanic on my watch.

My service on QE2 came to an end on the fifth of August 1973 when she docked once again at Ocean Terminal in Southampton. Rather than take the train home for a period of leave, I invited my family for a tour of this magnificent ship which they readily accepted. After the tour we had lunch in the officer's dining saloon and then I packed for the journey home.

I was sorry to leave QE2, but pleased to have had the opportunity to be a small part of her history.

Norway Cruise

Chapter 14

Warsash Interlude

Returning home after four months aboard QE2, I began a pleasant period of leave. Being with family and friends again for four weeks, the time passed quickly and all too soon I was on the move. This time however, I was not packing to travel overseas.

Having now completed fourteen months actual sea time, my progress towards qualification for a second mate certificate of competency required a return to the School Of Navigation at Warsash. So, on the 12th of September 1973, I began an intensive residential course of study.

No morning runs or parading at the sound of a bugle this time around. Instead, hours spent practising the solution of spherical triangles used in great circle navigation, and learning collision regulations verbatim filled each day. We studied ship construction, ship stability, and applied complex formulas to determine the minimum diameter of steel wire rope that could safely be used to lift a particular load. Receiving morse code by flashing light was considered essential as all ships were required to carry an Aldis lamp. Tests were frequent and included learning the meanings of the International Code Of Signals using flags. Coloured magnets on a blackboard were used to test our knowledge of different types of vessel and their aspect when seen at night.

In addition to several rowing boats, the school operated three larger vessels named Somerset, Halcyon and Stubbington. Somerset was a powered yacht used for radar training and plotting.

Occasionally, I would be part of the crew aboard Somerset for a night exercise to Weymouth.

Although time spent at the school was intense, most evenings included a visit to one of the local pubs. The Great Harry, Silver Fern and Rising Sun were never short of customers after the evening meal. The school had its own bar, but was rarely able to compete with the pubs at the far end of Newtown Road. Our own bar justified itself when a disco evening was arranged. Local girls were invited well in advance and the take-up was beyond expectations. This put me in a tight spot as a certain attractive Kathy Edwards indicated she was free to meet up with me the following day. But the following day, a Sunday, was already planned. I had previously volunteered for a charity long distance rowing exercise to the Isle Of Wight and return. The rowing team had been selected and I couldn't possibly let them down now. However, in exchange for as much beer as he could drink in one night, I was able to persuade one of my friends to take my place in the boat.

Fortunately my friend was quite a lightweight at beer drinking so the exchange ran to my advantage. I continued to meet up with Kathy regularly during the remaining weeks at Warsash and into my following leave. However, I had to accept that being away from the U.K. for months at a time was never conducive to a lasting relationship, and that fact would be repeated several times during my sea-going years.

Having a free afternoon once a week to pursue a sport was optional, and I chose to go into Southampton with a couple of friends to improve my swimming endurance. One of the criteria for joining the Merchant Navy was evidence of swimming ability. Up until that time, I could only produce a twenty-five yard school swimming certificate. It had been accepted as sufficient but I often wondered what use it might be in an emergency at sea. So during my time at Warsash, I undertook the Amateur Swimming Association survival courses and passed both bronze and silver standard. I felt confident enough to apply for the gold standard but time was not on my side.

Certificates for fire-fighting, efficient deck hand, lifeboatman and first aid were all considered essential before returning to sea, and these were all incorporated into the school's curriculum.

Fire-fighting involved being pushed into a smoke-filled, steel mock-up of a twin-deck ship's hold. Without breathing apparatus, we were expected to find our way out. Next was a similar exercise using breathing apparatus to locate and rescue a dummy. This was after fires had been lit inside the structure long enough to make the steel too hot in places to touch. Some of the students found the experience too claustrophobic and had to re-take the trial at a later date.

Qualifying as an efficient deck hand was equivalent to an able seaman rating without the sea time. In effect, it meant that if the student failed to progress any further, he could still follow a career at sea as a deck rating. I don't reckon I'll ever forget how to splice rope or tie a bowline knot.

The lifeboatman's course was held in Southampton docks and was an opportunity to demonstrate an ability to control a ship's lifeboat under oars and sail. It was not as easy as it sounds, and provided onlookers with amusement as many a hapless student engaged in a comedy of errors.

Thus armed with a folio of certificates, and confident at last that I could be an asset to a ship's complement, I went on leave at the conclusion of the course at the School Of Navigation. I knew that I was due to return to sit exams in a year or so, but for now I was looking forward to another adventure.

It was the 14th of December, and with a bit of luck I might get to spend Christmas at home.

Chapter 15

Luminetta

After the rigours of three months spent at Warsash, being able to spend Christmas 1973 at home was a welcome break. However, it was not to last.

In the second week of January 1974, I flew out to Gibraltar to join my next ship, Luminetta.

Approaching Gibraltar from the air was an unexpected experience. With only sea in sight from the small cabin windows on either side of the aeroplane, I watched as we lost height until it seemed as if we were going to ditch into the Mediterranean. The landing gear had been lowered but there was no land!

Reassuringly, tarmac appeared at the last moment and almost simultaneously there was a squeal as rubber made rather heavy contact with it. Jet engines screamed in reverse thrust and heavy braking brought the aircraft to a walking pace in seconds. My seatbelt had done its job and prevented me from cuddling the seat in front. As the aircraft swung to the left, I could see there was only a very short piece of runway before the narrow beach on the western side of the isthmus. I wondered how many aircraft wrecks may be found in the sea at the end of such a ridiculously short runway.

I had flown out in company with the uncertificated third mate - whose name eludes me, - and another deck cadet, Stuart Trundle. Both looked as white as I felt when we disembarked.

As we walked towards the terminal building, we were welcomed to Gibraltar by a large sign which read 'Welcome to Gibraltar'. Being January, the air was cool but the sun was shining brightly in a cloudless blue sky - a pleasant alternative to the damp, dull U.K. we had left behind.

An agent for the shipping company met us in the arrivals lobby and informed us that Luminetta's arrival had been delayed. So instead of transferring straight to the ship, we found ourselves as guests at The Rock Hotel.

For the next few days I was a tourist and managed to see pretty much everything that was worth seeing on this outpost of ancient British conquest. The history was fascinating. The town was compact and quite congested. Walking anywhere involved steep climbs or descents. Even the view from my hotel window was of a sheer rock face preventing sunlight from entering the room.

On one of my outings with Stuart, I witnessed one of the celebrated baboons snatch a bunch of keys from the hand of a tourist, scamper off and hurl the keys over a cliff wall. Seconds later we heard a faint splash.

The Rock Hotel had a fine-looking swimming pool which invited testing. There were few other guests due to the time of year so Stuart and I took advantage. The sun was shining but Stuart wrapped himself in a thick towel as the air temperature was extremely crisp. I expected the water to be quite cool but also knew the best way to enter the water was by an inspiring dive from the deep end. I believed that would impress Stuart as he had voiced his reservations.

When I hit the water the shock was extreme. I managed a few strokes to gain the surface but felt I was beginning to pass out. Luckily, I made it to the nearby steps and staggered to where my towel was waiting.

"Your turn" I uttered to Stuart - but he could see I was shivering violently and so declined.

I made mental note that if I ever had to abandon ship, I would take as much warm clothing as I could manage.

On the 12th of January, Luminetta berthed at the oil terminal in Gibraltar and my 'holiday' ended.

Luminetta was a tanker. Not one of the monsters that carried crude oil to refineries, but one that was designed specifically to transport the refined product.

I knew little about tankers and this was going to be a steep learning curve. Cunard, being a multi-fleet company, obviously wanted me to learn as much about the different vessels they operated as could be crammed into a four-year cadetship.

I learned very quickly that this type of tanker was little more than a floating bomb - particularly during discharge as the fuel to air mixture in the tanks became highly explosive. The day I joined her, Luminetta was discharging a full cargo of high octane petroleum. The most dangerous kind.

The Chief Officer, yet another Scot, made it very clear to Stuart and I that the slightest naked flame could turn Luminetta into a massive fireball. Smoking was prohibited. The dangers inherent in tankers was partly offset by a highly enhanced rate of pay. Except, of course, for cadets.

Scuppers at the ship's side had been covered with cement boxes to prevent the escape of any cargo into the dock water in the event of a spillage. Armed with a hammer and cold-chisel, the chief demonstrated how sparks could be generated by actually removing one of the boxes. If ever I needed convincing that only madmen applied to crew tankers......

We left Gibraltar without being vaporised and were instructed in the cleaning of the empty tanks as soon as land was lost to sight.

Thirty-three tanks with between two and four Butterworth lids per tank. Each lid had three enormous acorn nuts securing it to the deck. Each nut had to be undone by hand to allow the cleaning machine to be lowered into the cavernous space below. Stuart and I were each given a giant ring-spanner of appropriate size and given the job of undoing said nuts. I quickly discovered that the only successful way to start the nut was to lie on the wet deck and kick the spanner with the rubber sole of my boot. After removing a dozen or so nuts, and with Stuart watching, I had to give up due to a searing pain in the right side of my body.

The Bosun appeared clutching a special tool for the job which required minimal effort to operate. At this point I formed the opinion that our Chief Officer was not well disposed towards cadets.

The following morning, I was unable to move. I was completely seized and it was a full four days before I could sit upright.

For the next twenty years I suffered with frequent back pain which I attribute to my time on Luminetta. It wasn't until a physiotherapist at Flint House, a police convalescent home, discovered two interlocking bones - which shouldn't have been - that the problem was rectified.

Being at sea was preferable to time spent at an oil terminal because there was a routine which allowed for some socialising and an opportunity to evade the constant smell of petrol. For days after leaving a port, the stink of gasoline clung to clothing regardless of washing. At least on the bridge there was fresh air, so that every opportunity was taken to practice navigation.

As soon as we berthed, all the deck officers and crew were engaged in the control of pumps and pipeline valves that had to be constantly monitored. When the loading and discharge had been completed, we were off again.

My time on Luminetta was not a period that I remember with joy. Two months seemed like six. Shuttling between oil terminals in the U.S.A. and Europe, with little chance of shore leave, and much of the fun associated with other types of ship a distant memory, I was glad when we finally berthed at South Shields on the River Tyne.

On the 13th of March 1974, Stuart and I were summoned to the Chief Officer's office. This was as unusual as it was unexpected. We knocked and went inside to find the chief sitting behind his desk with his arms folded. With a solemn expression and a penetrating stare, he announced that we were both sacked! We looked at each other and then back to the chief. Ever-so-slowly, a grin started to spread across his face. It was his way of telling us that we were to pack and proceed on leave.

Maybe he did have a sense of humour - albeit very dry - after all.

Chapter 16

ACT 6

With a name that could be confused with a scene from a theatrical play, ACT 6 was a container ship operated by Associated Container Transportation. Unsurprisingly, it was the sixth vessel in that fleet. Also unsurprisingly, Cunard had an investment interest in this transport revolution.

Hence it was, that on the 22nd of April 1974, and following a pleasant five weeks of home leave, I travelled by train and taxi to Tilbury Docks.

At this time, containerisation of cargoes was in its infancy, and when I arrived at the recently constructed container port, I was amazed by the sight that greeted me. Massive specialist cranes known as 'portainers', straddler vehicles on towering legs, and gigantic stacks of steel boxes that were neatly arranged on the vast concrete apron heralded the future of global shipping.

ACT 6 was moored alongside this apron amidst a hive of activity. Twenty-foot containers were being lowered into holds situated ahead of the accommodation superstructure, as I struggled with suitcases up the narrow aluminium gangway. Once aboard, I located the chief officer who allowed me thirty minutes to unpack and change into working kit before making an appearance on deck.

My original working kit of dungarees and heavy cotton shirt had been worn out and was now replaced with the ubiquitous boiler suit and hard hat. I had learned that a boiler suit was far more practical and moreover, could usually be acquired without cost from the engine room stores.

That first day was extremely busy but also extremely interesting. On deck, there were no derricks, winches, masts, ringbolts, or the miles of wire rope that would be found on a traditional cargo ship. Instead, deep holds with guide rails swallowed up containers as they were lowered by the giant 'portainer' cranes. High above, I could see the driver of the crane looking down through a transparent panel as he positioned each container precisely over the guide rails.

The chief officer gave me a twenty-minute guided tour of the shipboard operation and then said: "Right I'm off - let me know of any problems. I'll be in my cabin".

That was my introduction to what was normally a hugely responsible job. Apparently, all the preparation and headache of loading plans had been replaced by boffins using electronic apparatus called computers.

I took my first meal break in the duty canteen where I was the only diner. The evening meal was ordered by telephone and was delivered by a steward. I was beginning to wonder where everyone was. I later discovered that I was the sole cadet on board and the mates were being entertained in the chief officer's cabin!

Eventually, the second mate made an appearance on deck just as the last containers were being loaded. He greeted me with "If you are quick, you can change and join the captain in the wheelhouse. We are sailing for Liverpool as soon as the pilot arrives".

Captain Carling was tall and slim with greying hair. I introduced myself and was pleasantly surprised to find him quite affable. The wheelhouse was wider than that on QE2 and was festooned with switches, dials and levers, all mounted on a long control console.

Casting off mooring ropes and manoeuvring with the aid of tugs, ACT 6 slowly passed through lock gates and into the Thames. I stayed on the bridge with the captain and chief officer until it was time to accompany the pilot to the waiting launch. On returning to the bridge I found the second mate had replaced the chief officer so realised it was after midnight. The captain said I should get some rest as I would be needed back on the bridge at 8 am.

It had been a long, tiring day and I went to my allotted cabin to finish unpacking and take a shower. I sat on my bunk to plan where to stow my worldly goods. There was a knock on the door and a steward had a cup of tea in his hand. "Seven o'clock sir! Will you be wanting breakfast?"

At least I didn't have to get dressed.

Wonderful city, Liverpool - at least the tiny bit I managed to see. Although we had two full days alongside, containers were waiting to be loaded and someone had to be constantly present on deck. Mostly me!

When the boxes were up to deck level, huge steel hatch covers were secured and more boxes were loaded on top. These had to be lashed down using a system of locking pins known as 'penguins', plus interlocking rods were also used. Some of the containers were refrigerated and had to be individually inspected for electrical connection. The deck officer's responsibility had burgeoned.

I did get one half-day ashore which enabled me to visit my grandmother who lived on The Wirral, just across the Mersey. I took the ferry and had Jerry Marsden's classic tune ringing in my ears during the crossing.

Before returning to the ship, I bought a cassette copy of Rod Stewart's 'Atlantic Crossing' and even now I am haunted by the track 'Sailing'.

An engineer cadet, Geoff Grouse, joined ACT 6 before we departed. Being a Liverpudlian himself, Geoff insisted on introducing me to a local delicacy. That last evening was spent in a local pub followed by a 'sausage dinner' at a chippy.

Never had gravy on chips before.

On the 26th of April 1974, a fully-laden ACT 6 made passage down the Mersey.

We were bound for Melbourne, Australia, a mere thirteen thousand miles away on the far side of our planet.

Chapter 17

ACT 6 Scene 2

This ship was different. It was German. Built by Bremer Vulkan and only thirty months old. Although still a cargo carrying vessel, once at sea, the cadet's routine was a steep contrast to that aboard Manipur or Port Caroline. There were no deck appliances to be chipped, wire brushed and painted. There were no wire ropes to be greased and the paint store was fully stocked and inventories completed. In fact, because ACT 6 was a recent build, everything appeared ship-shape from the start. Besides, most maintenance was contracted out to companies that completed anything needed whilst in port.

What was a deck cadet to do? I understood the reason for my employer to post me to this ship as a sole 'deck sprog', but the concept was lost on me at first. It hadn't yet dawned that this was the future of cargo shipping, and experience on this, one of the first class of container ships, could be invaluable in the future.

"Right, what can I find for you today?" said the chief officer, silhouetted in the doorway of my cabin on that first day out of Liverpool. It was six-thirty am.

"Be on the bridge before eight. You can assist the third mate".

So after a decent breakfast, and in full uniform, I went to the bridge to start a very pleasant month of eight to twelve watches which was to last the full passage to Melbourne in Australia.

Between 1967 and 1975, the Suez Canal was closed to shipping following the Six-Day War between Israel and Egypt. Fifteen merchant ships and their crews remained trapped in The Great Bitter Lake, including our own Port Invercargill. I was later to sail with the chief officer of the Port Invercargill and he told me of life marooned on a rusting hulk in sweltering heat and with a full cargo of rotting meat and apples!

Anyway, as that poor man and a skeleton crew were suffering aboard that trapped floating skip, ACT 6 continued around The Cape of Good Hope and into the South Indian Ocean.

The weather, which is always of paramount importance to a mariner, had been kind so far, but all that was set to change as we tried to maintain a great circle course from South Africa to Melbourne.

Being May, the relatively placid South Atlantic Ocean gave way to high winds and a heavy swell as The Cape of Good Hope receded into the distance. This was the beginning of winter in the southern hemisphere.

Great circle sailing is quite a challenge to navigation as it requires constant alterations of course to maintain the most direct path between two distant places on the earth's surface. The third mate and I would work out the course changes to be made every noon using the lost art of spherical trigonometry. Our calculations would be compared and were usually surprisingly close. Which was a relief, as Captain Carling would examine our jottings before making a final course decision. Nowadays of course, all this is done by satellite navigation, so the current crop of marine navigators have a comparatively easy time, I imagine.

The weather worsened, ACT 6 began rolling and pitching heavily in the driving wind and swell. Since the accommodation structure and hence the bridge, were sited well aft of the container deck, the vibration from the Stal Laval, epicyclic, double-reduction geared turbines was omnipresent and uncomfortable. The mountainous seas caused the single propeller to regularly rise out of the water and cause considerable shuddering as the turbines began to race. Sleep became scarce and even mealtimes suffered as galley staff tried their best to cope in the conditions.

During the bridge watches, any navigational calculations were hand written in pencil into a sight book that each of the watch keepers kept. These were personal items and I have retained some of mine. On ACT 6, however, the vibrations were so extreme that writing was an art in itself and much of the work indecipherable. Sometimes that could be an advantage - particularly in the case of a hastily corrected error prior to inspection by the captain.

It was our captain that made the decision to abandon great circle sailing due to the southerly latitudes we were ploughing towards. Good decision I thought. I would have done the same myself. No point in being unnecessarily uncomfortable for the sake of a few hundred miles. And besides, a straight line on a Mercator chart was much easier to follow, and obviated all those complicated calculations. By this time however, I considered myself almost expert.

Not all my time was spent assisting the third mate. As a cadet, I still had other work to perform on board. Life boat cleaning and maintenance, together with all other safety appliances was traditionally handed to cadets. Without any assistance, this took up quite a large part of my time when off watch. I also needed to keep my journal and work book up to date for frequent inspection by the chief officer. This was a condition of my company agreement and was evidence of experience and progress.

Melbourne eventually loomed into sight and I was on hand to meet the pilot for the passage up the Yarra. On mooring alongside the container terminal, cargo discharge started almost immediately. A swift change into hard hat and boiler suit, and I was soon on deck watching those huge containers being whisked off to their eagerly awaited destinations. No one on board knew the exact contents of the boxes unless it was particularly hazardous, but my guess was that there weren't any boomerangs or crocodile handbags.

Melbourne was no doubt one of those magnificent cities that I had read about on the outward voyage, but like our stay in Liverpool, time was short and shore leave shorter. I did get to see as much as time allowed but any city in wet wintry weather is never at its best.

On to Sydney then and an equally short stay before crossing the Tasman Sea to New Zealand.

I was beginning to conclude that container ships weren't for me. I joined the Merchant Navy to see the world - and not just the sea. I didn't know at the time that I was destined to see a lot more of both - and Antipodean ports, with all they had to offer - would be well explored in the future.

From Auckland, I wrote a postcard to my school pal Paul Wood. I have known Paul since my days at Alleyne's Grammar School in Stevenage. He was a survivor of Mister Burrage's purges and although we went our separate ways after leaving school, we have remained firm friends ever since. I include Paul's charming wife, Sue, who encourages me to continue with these scribblings.

Amazingly, Paul produced the very postcard I had sent to him all that time ago on a recent visit. The card was dated 11th of June 1974.

Equally amazing, but set back in a different time zone, was an announcement made to me by Captain Carling as we crossed the Tasman Sea en route to Kiwi Land.

"Nick, I've been notified by head office that we shall lose our third mate on arrival in Auckland. The company have proposed a replacement to be flown out but I have suggested that you are more than up to the job. How do you feel about that?"

Blimey, I thought. Am I really up to it so soon?

"I'll give it a go sir" I nervously replied.

Chapter 18

ACT 6 Scene 3

And so it was, that on the 25th of June 1974, I was promoted to third mate aboard ACT 6.

All of a sudden, I was no longer the 'deck sprog'. I was a watch-keeping officer with almost superhuman powers and, for eight hours of each day, in sole charge of a massive, shiny, new container ship.

I could even give instructions to crew members without quibble. I was twenty years old.

The homeward passage from New Zealand took us across the vast Pacific Ocean towards Panama. Each morning I would take a sun sight to obtain a position line. At noon, when the sun was at its highest in the sky, I took another altitude from the sun to fix our latitude. By running up the earlier position line I was able to obtain the ship's position. This would be corroborated by the second mate who took over the watch at midday.

Between navigational calculations, there were periods of inactivity on the bridge. Often, I would stand in the sun on a bridge wing just listening to the thrum of the engines and the sound of the sea water race passing along the ship's side. And all the time, I was being paid!

The view ahead was quite poor. Line of sight was hampered by the stacked containers which rose almost as high as the wheelhouse windows. Whilst on watch, my paramount responsibility was the safety of the ship. With forward visibility limited, and with our radar set being used only for coastal navigation or emergencies, I developed an automatic instinct to frequently scan the horizon from one beam to the other.

Lookouts were usually only posted during the hours of darkness, so most of the four-hour watch was spent in solitude. I didn't mind at all. In fact by practising 'lateral thinking' I was able to mentally shorten time considerably. It is a phenomena that takes some explaining! There would be occasional visits from Captain Carling or our 'sparks', but I was equally happy with or without company. Even today, I don't feel the need for constant socialising.

The Pacific is my favourite ocean. For two weeks, we steamed at twenty knots without seeing much apart from dolphins, flying fish and the odd albatross. Occasionally, another ship would be sighted on the horizon and I would attempt communication via our VHF radio set. If the watch keeper on the other vessel was on the ball, then we would have a short discussion. More often however, there would be no reply. Sometimes I wondered if they were keeping a watch at all!

The sea was generally as smooth as glass with just a slight swell. The night sky was unlike anything that most people experience. All heavenly bodies (stars, planets, etcetera), were at their brightest and shooting stars common. A full moon would complete the spectacle.

The weather was not always perfect. Quite often we would enter a squall, and rain would hammer in sheets against the bridge front. When that happened, I would switch on our pair of 'Kent Clear View' screens. These were circular plates of glass set into the wheelhouse windows which spun at high revs, flicking away raindrops and aiding visibility.

The Pacific is dotted with small islands. A patch of cloud on the horizon of an otherwise cloudless sky would often indicate the presence of land below. From compass bearings of the cloud edges, and related to the location of land on our Admiralty charts, it was possible to check the ship's position. Quite a useful navigational aid.

Once east of the Galapagos Islands, a concentration of shipping began to build on the approach to The Panama Canal - the South American Isthmus was only one day's steaming away - and so preparation for arrival intensified.

Arrival Panama, and the prospect of mail from home! Always eagerly awaited, mail was the only link we had with family and friends for sometimes months on end. Another example of how much larger the world seemed then. Hastily written letters were posted, hinting at possible leave.

Transiting the canal, which was always a fascinating experience, indicated that we were half way to our European destination.

Into the Caribbean Sea and laying course lines on the chart to steer the ship safely through the island chains, became our next priority. The second mate had overall responsibility for selecting the courses to follow and these were often altered during the watch to avoid any hazards. This massive ship could be turned by simply rotating a knurled knob in the centre of the gyro compass.

Our Atlantic crossing passed without incident, but the weather worsened as ACT 6 entered the Western Approaches. Off the north-west coast of France, in the vicinity of Ushant, there are numerous outcrops of rock. Among these, 'The Minkies' are probably the most notorious, having claimed hundreds of ships and their crews in preceding years. I recall seeing waves breaking on this expansive cluster of jagged black rock and wondering what could happen if a navigational error or engine failure put us among them. For years after leaving the sea, the sight often haunted me at night when sleep was being evasive.

As luck would have it, we managed to avoid all the hazards to shipping that litter The English Channel and kept to the eastbound navigational waterway as far as Dover. Alterations of course took us into the Thames Estuary, past the old Shivering Sands anti-aircraft complex that had been erected to deter the Luftwaffe during the Second World War, and upstream to Tilbury.

On arrival, a change of crew, including our captain, was organised, but I was to remain with the ship for the coastal discharge ports. It was the 22nd of July 1974, so I wasn't too surprised as I had only clocked up three months sea time since joining ACT 6.

My turn came, however, on the 31st of July when I was suddenly given home leave.

No matter how well a mariner develops an attachment to a ship or its crew, the offer of leave will always take priority. At least it did in my case.

Although my leave was to last less than a month, it was a month that was to introduce me to another exciting form of adventure and independence which I have never been able to shake off.

But then why should I? Motor-cycling can become a life-style in itself!

Chapter 19

Wheels

To be on leave for most of August 1974 was the catalyst for change. Living at home was pleasant and convenient but relying on public transport hampered my independence. I had a bicycle that I built for myself whilst at school using an old Claude Butler frame, but its single gear was hard work and carrying capacity limited. What I really needed was a new bicycle. With an engine!

My promotion had increased my salary and so I began studying the market. My friend Bern had ridden motorbikes for some years, and another friend, Mark, decided it was time for him to become mobile as well.

Bern's advice was to buy British, as our own industry built better quality motorbikes than the Japanese invaders whose imports were now flooding into the U.K. At this time, Bern was ardently anti-Japanese, and would relish every opportunity to criticise their two-wheeled offerings.

The dilemma was frustrated by the fact that our industry was only producing large capacity bikes, and I was restricted by my newly-acquired provisional licence to a maximum of 250 cc.

The look of horror on Bern's face when I turned up outside his house on my brand new, orange Honda CB 125, will remain entrenched in my memory.

It didn't matter much to me - I was properly mobile at last - and beginning to experience the excitement of riding wherever I wanted at close to sixty miles per hour!

My considered choice of motorbike was influenced by the fact it was a four-stroke engine which to me sounded so much better than the two-stroke 'howlers' that were everywhere. It was also relatively cheap at £125 brand new, but most of all, it just looked handsome.

I was not alone in my choice of bike. Within a week, Mark appeared outside my house on exactly the same model - albeit a different colour.

Spending August riding to nowhere in particular just for the fun of being able to ride to nowhere in particular was a revelation. The weather was good, I had friends to ride with and even a run to the coast and back was achievable within a day.

The Lemsford Transport Cafe, a popular biker haunt that remained open all night, and the Chequers pub at Woolmer Green, became regular destinations. I made a lot of new friends among the biking community and there was even talk about starting our own local motorcycle club.

Towards the end of August I took a telephone call from Mike Taylor who was a personnel manager with Cunard. Mike requested that I be at Heathrow airport on the 26th to take a flight out to Melbourne to join my next ship - Port Nicholson.

It was becoming commonplace to fly to and from our ships wherever they may be in order to allow officers to take overdue leave or sometimes for personal reasons.

Mike was at pains to point out that he was aware I was due back at The School Of Navigation in Warsash to study for my final examinations at the beginning of the new year. He would try to pull the necessary strings, but I should pack for at least six months in any case.

I suppose being desk bound in a London office made Mike a little envious of his 'charges' being able to travel at short notice to almost any exotic destination on the planet.

His parting shot was to inform me that the flight to Melbourne would take thirty six hours and be via Rome, Dubai, Singapore and Darwin.

So on the 26th August, I boarded a Vickers Super VC-10 at Heathrow and buckled in for the marathon flight.

The take off was perfect and soon the aircraft had gained height and was heading off into the sun.

That was rather disturbing. It was already mid afternoon and I had expected the pilot would have banked onto a southerly course. I waited for the course change that didn't materialise.

Twenty minutes later, the captain made an announcement on the intercom.

He pointed out that the weather ahead was clear and we may see the south coast of Ireland from the right hand windows in about thirty minutes time. Our arrival time at J.F.K. in New York was on schedule.

Ireland! New York! Blimey, I've caught the wrong flight. This was catastrophic! I began to flush hot and cold with worry. How could this possibly happen?

Another ten minutes passed before I summoned the nerve to explain my predicament to the air-stewardess.

She listened with a frown on her forehead, but all credit to her for her reasoned reply:

"Never mind" she said, "I'll just have a word with the pilot and see if I can get him to turn round".

I was instantly confused. Then, with a smile, she added:

"There is no mistake - we are flying to Melbourne - but just the other way round. I suggest you give your personnel manager a piece of your mind when you next speak".

Now reassured, I settled into the rest of the flight, chasing the parallel sun as we headed west at a similar speed.

We landed at New York, Los Angeles, Honolulu, Fiji, Sydney and finally, Melbourne.

I determined that I would speak to Mike at my next opportunity - he needed to get out more!

Chapter 20

Port Nicholson

They don't build them like that any more. Haven't done for years. Here was a magnificent, traditional refrigerated cargo ship of the famous Port Line. Quality! Port Nicholson exuded quality.

Built in 1962 at Belfast by Harland and Wolff - the same shipbuilders responsible for Titanic - she was to spend her entire service life with Port Line.

Now it was my turn to be a small part of the history surrounding Port Nicholson.

So it was, that on the 27th of August 1974, I boarded Port Nicholson as she was working cargo in Melbourne on the south coast of Australia.

As a recently promoted third officer, I was shown to a cabin on the forward starboard side of the accommodation block. This was a single cabin with a bunk bed that could be made into a double. There was also a day bed which acted as a settee set at right angles to the bunk. The significance of the design allowed for a choice of sleeping positions depending on the motion of the ship when a heavy sea was encountered. The cabin had its own en-suite shower room with full facilities and apart from the rather dull wall covering, appeared very comfortable. The view forward from the window covered the entire fore deck where I could see the cargo operations.

When I had unpacked and met other officers and crew, I soon learned that Port Nicholson was a rather sick old lady in need of extensive engine repairs.

After all cargo had been discharged on the Australian coast, we set an interesting series of courses that took us through the Coral Sea, east of The Great Barrier Reef and into the Solomon Sea heading northwards.

We passed many islands which could be identified using Admiralty Charts and Sailing Directions. The latter were a series of books which included diagrams of various coastlines and interesting facts about the islands themselves. These had been compiled over many years and I found them fascinating. The original contributors were often explorers themselves, employed by the British Admiralty, and must have experienced eventful lives. No other nation ever produced such detailed records.

At this time of year for the Southern Hemisphere, the weather was surprisingly pleasant. The seas were calm and brilliantly blue, the sky often cloudless.

However, our engineers were constantly worrying about the condition of the engines and requesting we maintain lower revs than usual. It occurred to me that if we were to suffer a catastrophic engine failure, what an idyllic part of the world we would be stranded in!

As it happened, the huge twin diesel engines maintained a steady beat as Port Nicholson passed over The Mariana Trench. At thirty six thousand feet, it is the deepest area of water on Planet Earth. Inexplicably, I felt an unjustified sense of relief when we had completed the crossing.

It was late September when we arrived at our destination.

The massive Kawasaki ship building and repair yard in Kobe, Japan was an impressive sight.

Before we had even entered the port, numerous small craft had brought Japanese shipyard workers out to the ship along with pilots. Port Nicholson was fully dry-docked and had her starboard propeller removed before the day was out. I was stunned at the speed in which the Japanese tackled the engine repairs.

I was able to wander around the dry dock at leisure and look up at the huge hull of my home from keel level. To watch the Japanese at work was inspiring, but I was happy to remain a spectator and move among the workers as if I understood fully what they were attempting to achieve. Perhaps they might have mistaken me for an inspector as they were embarrassingly polite.

For the duration of our stay in Kobe, I took, as always, every opportunity to get ashore and explore.

Two significant memories clearly remain.

Firstly, it was in one of the large shopping malls that I was able to buy the latest 35mm single-lens-reflex camera. An Olympus OM-1 body in black. At the time, I couldn't afford the 50mm lens to go with it so my only images from that era remain poor quality. It would be six months before I acquired a lens but after that my interest and proficiency in photography grew. That camera became a close personal friend for the next thirty years.

The second significant memory refers to a very cute Japanese girl I met on one of my solo explorations. Kozuka Fuji was my age and working in a cafe that I had ventured into. As the only European customer, I suppose I attracted attention and was pleasantly surprised to be served by an attractive local girl who was keen to practice her very broken English.

I was even more surprised when she offered to show me parts of Kobe that I never knew existed.

Unhesitatingly, I accepted her friendly offer and as a result, will retain very fond memories of my time spent in Kobe with Kozuka.

Sadly, the super-efficient Kawasaki workforce repaired Port Nicholson in only five days and it was time to say goodbye. On departure I had a strong premonition that I would return one day.

To date, my premonition remains unfulfilled.

Or could there just be an element of confused truth……?

Although I could not have known at that time, a very similar occurrence in another part of the world was to change my life five years into the future.

Chapter 21

Mutton Maid

With her engines now repaired, Port Nicholson retraced most of the courses that had brought us to Kobe from Australia. However, on approaching The Great Barrier Reef, we altered our heading to a south easterly direction as we had instructions to make for New Zealand.

The geographical Port Nicholson is the name given to the natural harbour which enabled the kiwi capital, Wellington, to develop into what it has become today.

Our ship was en route to her spiritual home.

Changing times were being felt throughout the shipping industry. Normally, we would expect to load lamb, fruit and dairy products for the European market.

But not this time.

Instructions from head office detailed that we would be taking a full cargo of mutton carcasses to a new customer - Russia!

The typical European housewife was always happy to buy New Zealand lamb since it had a reputation for quality. Mutton however, was not so popular with her, so a new market had to be found for the New Zealand mutton market.

The typical Russian housewife, it seemed, had no qualms about buying mutton - or any edible produce - for that matter.

Our New Zealand coastal was the usual riot of parties on board in the traditional Port Line manner.

Leaving that wonderful country and its inhabitants on the 1st of November was always going to be a wrench, but we had a job to do and the Nicholson set course for a destination no one on board had ever heard of - Nakhodka. A special Admiralty chart covering the East Siberian coast was delivered just prior to departure.

The 'Nick' was full to capacity with frozen mutton which provided the nickname 'Mutton Maid'.

Heading north, we entered the tropics and about a week of sunshine. Our course took us through the Soloman and Caroline Islands which appeared as they would in films about The South Pacific with their palm trees, reefs and atolls.

Whilst in New Zealand, I took the opportunity to buy some reading material for the northward voyage to the Russian east coast. Among the books I thought would be educational was a copy of Alexander Solzhenitsyn's 'The Gulag Archipelago'. Until reading of his experiences in the Soviet labour camps as a result of his dissident views, I had no Idea how cruel a regime could be.

A note inside the book's cover referred to it being prohibited material in Russia. This worried me a little as I had been left with the impression that anyone caught infringing Russian law could find themselves arrested and sentenced to a labour camp for even minor misdemeanours.

My mind was made up. As we crossed the Mariana Trench for the third time, I placed the book in a small canvas bag together with a heavy iron shackle and secured it with polypropylene rope.

Creeping to the ship's port side, I hurled the package into the sea and watched as it instantly sank. At a depth of six miles, I thought it unlikely the book would ever be recovered.

We were now well into November 1974 and as we headed north, the temperature began to plummet. The engines were fixed, but the steam heating system was playing up, and for several days the accommodation block was literally freezing. Going on watch, I would wear the pyjamas (that my dear mum had insisted I packed) underneath my uniform blues and thick woollen pullover. It was not enough. To venture onto the bridge wing to take an azimuth bearing was painful. Not many bearings were taken as a result. Mental note made to obtain proper thermals.

Port Nicholson anchored off Yokohama in Japan for engine spares and documents to be brought out to the ship. No going alongside this time so a swift trip down to visit Kozuka in Kobe was out of the question.

I was given the dubious honour of navigating the 'Mutton Maid' through The Tsugaru Kaikyo. This was the strait which separated mainland Honshu from Hokkaido Island to the north.

Darkness had fallen when I took the watch just before eight o'clock (bells) as we approached the eastern entrance to the strait. This rather narrow stretch of water is notorious as one of the busiest shipping lanes in the world. However, when the Japanese fishing fleets, which materialise at this time of evening, are added to the equation, then this becomes the most congested and confused waterway on Earth. Even the captain looked worried during his frequent visits to the wheelhouse. The view from the bridge resembled Blackpool illuminations due to all the other vessel's navigation lights and the powerful Japanese fishing boat lights.

Alterations of course were frequent and nobody was more surprised than me when we cleared the strait without hitting anything significant.

From here, we crossed The Sea Of Japan heading for the port of Nakhodka, which is located to the south east of Vladivostok.

Approaching the Russian coast, we experienced a rare maritime phenomena - Arctic Sea Smoke. This was caused by bitterly cold air coming into contact with relatively warm sea water. The air in contact with the sea surface warms, rises and condenses to form a type of fog. Going on my morning watch I was amazed at being able to see over a blanket of thick, swirling fog which rendered the sea surface invisible. Any small craft would be in real trouble in such conditions.

Just after midnight on the 16th of November, 'Mutton Maid' dropped anchor in Zaliv Amerika, the bay on which Nakhodka is situated. A powerful coastal searchlight swept the entire bay which seemed rather unnecessary, but we were in Russian waters now. I was reminded of some of Solzhenitsyn's descriptions in his book, and although our steam heating was working again, I experienced the odd shiver.

We were two miles from the port, but as soon as the anchor windlass was secured, a Russian gunboat came alongside. We were boarded on arrival by a group of uniformed, fur-hatted and armed border guards who insisted on carrying out a search on selected members of our crew.

I felt vindicated in having committed Alexander's book to the deep.

Although nothing incriminating had been found, I think the entire crew had been put on edge.

Later that day I heard our Chief Engineer explaining his indignation over lunch. He was at pains to describe the border guards as being at least six feet tall by three feet wide and all women!

Russia was going to be a unique experience for the complement of 'Mutton Maid'.

Night Time Navigation

Chapter 22

Nakhodka

On the evening of the 16th of November 1974, during my watch, Port Nicholson weighed anchor, and with a Russian pilot on board, moved to her berth in the East Siberian port of Nakhodka.

Light snow flurries reduced visibility as did the arctic sea smoke. It was bitterly cold and I was wearing every stitch of warm clothing I possessed. My pyjamas had never seen such use.

Once we were securely tied up alongside the berth, I had to venture on deck to open the heavy steel MacGregor hatch coverings over the holds to be worked.

I needn't have bothered because the workforce was nowhere in sight. After about an hour of waiting I was about to close them again but it made more sense to me to leave them open since the air temperature was much lower than the refrigerated hold temperatures. The chief officer, contemplating my decision over a glass of malt whisky in his heated cabin, agreed. A crew member, designated as a watchman, would inform us if any Russians came aboard.

Early next morning a group of weary-looking Russians turned up and shuffled along the deck into number two hold. An ancient dockside crane creaked into life and swung an enormous iron bucket which was then heavily dropped onto the surface of the mutton carcasses causing significant damage to them. No one seemed to mind. Laboriously, the gang of Russians in the hold began throwing carcasses into the bucket in a haphazard fashion. I began to wonder how long they anticipated the discharge to last if this was their A-team at work.

We could be here for weeks. Nobody seemed to know and none of the Russians spoke English.

Eventually, an agent came aboard who could speak sufficient english to confirm a stay of at least two weeks. Two weeks! Anywhere else in the world and we would expect a full discharge in a single port of two to four days.

So what now? There was very little supervision to be done on deck as the unloading was agonisingly slow. Was a trip ashore worthwhile? The agent confirmed that we could go ashore but was at a loss to offer any suggestions as to why we should want to. Nakhodka was a large port with town to match but it seemed there was nothing for foreign visitors to visit.

I canvassed the other officers about exploring but their lack of enthusiasm was total.

I concluded that I would have to venture into Siberia alone.

Perhaps alone sounds a little negative. I had a travel companion. Along with my late copy of 'The Gulag Archipelago', I was pleased that I had had the foresight to buy a pocket copy of the Berlitz Russian phrasebook before leaving New Zealand. Now was the time to test it.

The agent advised me of where I could catch a bus into the main part of town. She added that If I wore my full uniform then I wouldn't be charged a fare. That wouldn't work in Southampton.

Blimey it was cold. The bridge thermometer had packed up at minus ten degrees. The dock and roadway to where I understood I would find a bus was icy and covered with a layer of snow.

I was shivering uncontrollably and was about to turn back when a bus hove into view. I was at the point where I could abort with honour, but at least the bus would be heated? Wouldn't it?

I stepped aboard and found the interior a bit of a crush. Standing room only. At the next stop more passengers squeezed aboard and to my amazement began handing me ten-kopek coins.

I tried to give them back but was rebuffed. Why would these people give me money? Did I look like a charity case? Had they seen my pyjamas? I discretely put the coins in my pocket.

When I had travelled several stops, I thought I saw some shops at the foot of a fairly tall building. I needed some warm clothing and decided this was a good enough place to get off. I was about to cross the road when a voice behind me asked "Where are you from?" in reasonable English.

I turned around and faced a young man of similar age, also in naval uniform.

"England" I replied in a rather surprised fashion.

Although it took a while to get acquainted, this was Sasha, a student of 'The Far East Marine School' in Nakhodka.

We spoke for maybe twenty minutes in that bitter cold and then Sasha invited me to his parent's flat nearby. Could I refuse? That might seem rude, and besides, I was shivering quite violently.

On the way to the flat, Sasha explained that a foreign visitor was rarely seen in Nakhodka and I formed the impression that I was a bit of a curiosity. He also explained that my pocketful of coins was due to me not understanding that it was customary for the bus passenger nearest the coin box to place other passenger's fares into it. That is how I had come to Sasha's notice.

How embarrassing! My ignorance had left me several roubles richer! How was I to know?

Sasha's parents lived in an apartment flat in one of the six-storey grey buildings that lined the main road. Both parents were extremely hospitable and within minutes a table had been laid for some sort of meal.

That meal consisted of salad, black bread, boiled eggs and vodka. Tea was optional.

Sasha and I talked in Anglo-Russian as best we could whilst his parents were asking numerous questions of Sasha. I picked up a boiled egg and began to peel it. It was raw! Sasha's dad laughed out loud and insisted on showing me how to swallow a raw egg followed by a full glass of vodka. A silence followed. I reluctantly copied what I had just witnessed and was complimented by a hearty slap on the back.

After the meal, Sasha accompanied me to a local store where I was able to buy a traditional fur hat and thick gloves. In return, I gave Sasha my uniform cap with Cunard badge by way of a souvenir. He was so pleased, he immediately replaced his own with it.

He showed me to the bus stop and waited until the correct bus arrived. There was a small crowd of locals also waiting. One of them had a small dog on a lead. Here was my chance. I looked up the necessary vocabulary in my Berlitz and pointed to the dog.

"Maleenky sobaka!" (small dog) I exclaimed rather more loudly than intended.

Everyone in the crowd stared at me and then began laughing. Was it my pronunciation?

Sasha and I had become good friends in just an afternoon, but when the bus came it was time to say goodbye to another individual that I would never meet again.

Chapter 23

Nakhodka Vodka

I rather wished I had asked Sasha for his contact details as I would have at least sent his family a Christmas card. Of course even that would be difficult as I would need to practice writing the Cyrillic alphabet. I also wondered if the Soviet authorities would accept incoming foreign mail.

My shore venture in Nakhodka was unique. None of the ship's company attempted shore leave and I considered the bitter cold a sufficient reason to now remain aboard for the duration.

The discharge of mutton continued at a snail's pace and I spent most of my cargo watch time in the heated deck office, only venturing outside when absolutely necessary. Joining me in the deck office at frequent intervals was the Russian foreman. His name was Valeri. Now Valeri was quite a jovial sort of character which was in stark contrast to most of his workforce. He would often appear at the same time as the tea and tab-nabs (usually biscuits) delivered by our steward.

Valeri's knowledge of the English language was matched by my knowledge of Russian, so much of the time was spent in trying to understand each other. It helped pass the time and with reference to my phrase book, I was starting to grasp some elements of this impossible language.

Another frequent visitor to the deck office was the female agent whose name I have forgotten.

One morning she delivered a crate of books to distribute among the crew. These were all English language copies of political dialogue extolling the virtues of the Soviet communist system. Understandably, there weren't many interested parties, but I was drawn to the volumes dedicated to the Russian participation in the 'Great Patriotic War'. The photographs were superb and it had been printed on high quality paper. These books would have been expensive to produce.

The agent became aware of my interest in the military history volumes, and from that point until we departed, I was deluged with similar books for the onward voyage.

One very cold night as the discharge was nearing completion, Valeri entered the deck office wearing an unusually heavy overcoat. "Nick, gdye stakhan?" he uttered excitedly.

I looked at him bewildered.

Valeri produced an enormous bottle of Stalichnaya vodka from the inside of his coat.

The penny dropped and I realised that he was asking for a glass. I obliged him and then he insisted I accompany him outside. Following him to the depths of number one hatch, Valeri called the gang over to a pile of mutton in one corner. This was out of the sight of the huge female crane driver who began shouting protestations at the gang who were taking an unauthorised break.

The group made themselves as comfortable as possible while Valeri opened the bottle. He filled the tumbler I had given him to the brim and handed it to me with a gesture that I should have the first glass. Perhaps the horrified look on my face was enough for him to retrieve the glass and drain the contents in one continuous swallow. Even the gang was impressed and they all repeated the procedure at their turn. All too quickly the glass was refilled and passed to me.

With a dozen pairs of Russian eyes waiting with anticipation, and with England's honour at stake, I declared "Na zdarovya!" (To health) and drank the quarter pint of Stalichnaya, albeit in several swallows. The Russians were delighted and the whole process was repeated.

My watch was due to finish at eight a.m. However, the ship's carpenter discovered the third mate standing at the ship's bow at six a.m., during the 'chippy's' morning tank soundings. Apparently, the third mate, who was wearing a thick Russian overcoat and fur hat, was staring at the Gora Sestra mountain from where searchlights were conducting their regular sweep of the bay.

Our 'chippy' suspected something was amiss and suggested I went to bed.

I know all this because it became a topic of discussion among the crew for weeks ahead.

At last, on the 3rd of December 1974, Port Nicholson departed Nakhodka in ballast.

We were bound for New Zealand which put the grins back on the faces of the entire crew.

That was until instructions from head office informed us that we were to load another full cargo of mutton. The discharge destination was undisclosed but we all knew it would be Russia again.

No other nation wanted the stuff!

Anyway, a week or two on the New Zealand coast was on offer first, and that was likely to heal any misgivings. It was mid-summer down in the Antipodes and that would be a welcome relief after the freezing temperatures we had all endured.

Fifteen days after leaving Nakhodka, we were in Timaru on South Island, where our first consignment of mutton was waiting for us. This should not be confused with some of the girlfriends that the less particular crew members had waiting for them.

Standards were normally very high!

On a more mundane note, I had requested that Fleet Personnel back in London seriously consider my request to be able to attend The School Of Navigation in Warsash.

I now had sufficient sea-time to apply for the Second Mate Certificate Of Competency examination. The new term would begin in early January so I knew I had little chance of being repatriated in time.

Our last loading port on the New Zealand coast was Whangarei on the north-east coast of North Island.

On a hot summer's morning on the 30th of December, having completed mooring to a berth, I was still on the bridge. The captain had gone below and left me to secure the wheelhouse and ring 'Finished With Engines'. I was very hot and looking forward to a shower before loading began.

The engine room telephone rang.

"Don't answer that!" came the captain's voice from behind.

I turned to see the captain in the wheelhouse doorway.

"The agent has just come aboard. There is a flight from the local air-strip in just over an hour and you are booked on it. Better get yourself packed quickly as the airfield is thirty minute's drive away".

This was head office's belated reply to my earlier request.

'Sparks' and the second mate threw all my belongings in my suitcases while I took a record-breaking shower. There was no time to say goodbye to everyone, but as I made my way down the gangway to the waiting taxi, a party had gathered to wish me luck. Among them was the purser.

"Shouldn't you give me my discharge book?" I asked of him.

The purser didn't reply but disappeared into the accommodation. Five minutes later, the book, duly stamped, was in my hand. However, it was five minutes I could ill afford.

My taxi driver seemed to enjoy the high speed race to the little airfield at Whangarei.

"It'll be okay, mate. They are expecting you - and if I know the crew, they'll wait a while".

At the airfield, I could see the twin-engined Fokker with its propellers turning and I had to run across grass to the open doorway. I hurled my suitcases into the opening and a stewardess's hand helped me aboard. We were airborne before I had fastened my seat belt.

Chapter 24

Return To Warsash

The little Fokker took only thirty minutes to reach Auckland.

Here, I transferred to a mighty Boeing 747 Jumbo Jet of Singapore Airlines for the marathon flight back to the U.K. Interestingly, our route included stops at Sydney, Darwin, Singapore, Dubai and Rome. In joining and leaving Port Nicholson, I had circumnavigated the earth by air.

I had only three full days of home leave before I was due to begin six months of intensive study. In addition to the Second Mates Certificate Of Competency qualification, I had also been enrolled into the National Certificate Of Nautical Science programme by the school.

I hadn't asked to. Perhaps they had faith.

On the 5th of January 1975, I arrived back at Warsash with mounting apprehension. The sheer volume of study required prior to sitting the exams in the summer seemed a forlorn hope. Having worked alongside deck officers at sea, I was always hugely impressed by their skill and knowledge. When I began my career, the title 'Cadet Eliason' had a long-term ring to it.

During that first week, my apprehension grew as I was introduced to the syllabus. I took some comfort from the fact that I was in the company of friends from previous courses who were equally stunned by the school's expectations.

Most evenings were spent in 'The Great Harry' or 'Silver Fern' pubs up in the village discussing stories that we all had accumulated. Reference to study was practically forbidden.

Home leave was permitted at weekends and I took advantage of going home for the first few. Considering I had only three days leave since the previous summer, I felt in denial.

It soon became evident that our precious weekends would be taken up in trying to grasp the detail of lectures from the previous week. I needed to learn to concentrate more and constantly revise ground already covered. The six months allocated for study was never going to be enough.

Now that I was the proud owner of a Honda motorcycle, it would be churlish not to use it for the Knebworth to Warsash commute. However, it was mid winter and I had no warm motorcycle kit.

My dad loaned me his old R.A.F. Irvin flying jacket and I still had pyjamas.

That first journey from home was an adventure in itself. I was a learner so had to avoid motorways. It was already getting dark when I set off, and to add to the winter cold, it began to drizzle twenty miles into my one hundred and five mile epic.

Travelling along unfamiliar roads in the dark, cold and wet, my ability to cover ground was reduced to an embarrassing crawl. The thick, fleece-lined Irvin jacket, whilst serving a useful purpose in a waterproof aeroplane during the war, was now absorbing the increasing rainfall, acting as a massive sponge and doubling in weight.

Somewhere near Basingstoke, on an unlit stretch of the A30, I felt I was nearing my endurance limit. The rain had penetrated all my clothing and the wind chill factor was contributing to the onset of hypothermia. All I could see was the rain falling in front of my own headlight and the slow passage of the broken white line in the middle of the road. I needed to get out of this weather.

Occasionally, miracles occur when you least expect them.

Set back from the A30 in a clearing among a wooded area on the westbound side of the road, I saw light illuminating a small parking area. This was 'The Happy Motorist' transport cafe.

Rated among moments of sheer relief, this remains near the top of my list.

Apart from three staff and one family sitting at a corner table, the cafe was empty. The female staff saw the state I was in and immediately produced a steaming mug of tea. I allowed myself thirty minutes to dry off before continuing the last forty miles of my miserable journey.

Four-and-a-half hours later, I bid farewell to 'The Happy Motorist'. It was still bitterly cold outside but the rain had eased and I was packed full of eggs, beans, sausages and chips.

When I finally limped into Warsash it was past midnight. The trip had taken almost ten hours but had taught me some valuable lessons. I made a point of always stopping at 'The Happy Motorist' whenever I was on the A30. Sadly, that oasis has long gone.

Having my own transport at the school proved a great asset. When not studying, which was more often than I could afford, it enabled me to maintain regular contact with a girl I met at one of the school's regular discos. Her name was Wendy Elizabeth Newton and she lived with her family in Schooling, a suburb of Southampton. We just happened to get on rather well.

Phil Haynes, a friend of mine studying at Warsash, also had access to a motorbike. Often in the evenings we would go out for a 'spin' in the local lanes before ending up at one of the pubs.

March the 18th 1975 was my 21st birthday. Phil insisted we celebrate the fact starting at 'The Great Harry' during lunchtime. We saved some time by travelling to the pub on our motorbikes. After all, we had some important lectures that afternoon that we couldn't afford to miss.

All track of time was lost when a group of students from the same course were already waiting at the pub with pints already on the bar. What an afternoon!

At around five o'clock when all lectures had finished for the day, Phil reckoned it would be a good idea to ride back to the school via the scenic route.

I followed and we were soon in familiar lanes. The pace quickened and I was beginning to think Phil had downed too many pints. Never gave the same thought to myself.

After ten miles or so, the inevitable happened. On a tight right-hand bend, I hit a pile of loose gravel. My bike high-sided and flung me through a thick, thorny hedge lining the left of the road.

As I passed through the hedge, my open-face helmet surrendered with the result that all exposed flesh was shredded by thorns. Apart from that, I had a comfortable landing in a ploughed field.

A kindly lady, out walking her dog, put her head through the hole I had just created in the hedge and asked If I was alright.

Back at Warsash, I was in a hurry to get showered and changed since I had promised Wendy a night out to remember. I could have cancelled, but a promise is a promise, and besides, it was my birthday.

And not just any old birthday - I was now twenty one years old and was expected to assume the responsibilities that maturity brings.

I counted just over forty separate cuts to my face but at least I managed to pick out the last of the thorns. My motorbike was a little worse for the afternoon's adventure but it still worked.

I was only a little late when I rang Wendy's doorbell.

The look of sheer horror she openly displayed when she answered and saw the pitiful state my face had deteriorated into, led me to conclude that perhaps I should have aborted after all......

Chapter 25

Summer Of '75

Early on the morning of the 4th of April 1975, whilst still dark, I kitted up in the warmest clothing I possessed, and endured the expedition home on my twisted and scarred Honda 125 motorbike.

The School Of Navigation was closing for an Easter break.

My priority for the interval was intensive study towards the forthcoming exams. However, studying motorcycle magazines and brochures took a disproportionate part of the time I had allocated.

To have transport and the freedom to use it, inevitably caused academic study to suffer.

Before returning to Warsash, I had replaced the Honda CB 125 with its bigger brother, a brand new Honda CB 250. Twin cylinders, more power and more speed. Altogether a bigger bike. Now I was really going places. It looked magnificent in blue metallic paint.

Bern still grumbled that it was Japanese, but my friend Mark agreed with my choice of upgrade.

So much so, that within a week, he had bought the same model but in green. Now we planned all sorts of adventures, but they would have to wait until my next leave in late July.

Wendy visited me in Knebworth for a very pleasant long weekend.

I returned to Warsash in style on the 21st of April. The weather had improved significantly and in addition to a brand new motorcycle, I had some decent motorcycle kit to go with it.

The following three months were indeed intense. There were so many different subjects that had to be mastered that I felt overwhelmed.

The National Certificate In Nautical Science was the first series of exams on the horizon and required passes in Mathematics, Applied Science, Navigation, Meteorology, Nautical Studies, Seamanship and Liberal Studies.

I didn't even know beforehand what Liberal Studies were.

As it happened, I was quite good at everything to do with navigation and put unbridled effort into understanding the principles behind the various navigational chart projections.

On the day of the navigation exam, three of the six questions were concerning chart projections.

All the other required subjects are now faded memories, but I must have satisfied the examination assessors as they saw fit to award me an Ordinary National Certificate In Nautical Science.

Working through the Second Mate's syllabus was tougher still. Apart from all the written exams held at the Board Of Trade building in Southampton, there was a requirement to appear before a seasoned Master Mariner for oral interrogation.

Collision regulations, all thirty-one of them, were expected to be learned verbatim. By comparison, the Highway Code would look like a volume from the Noddy library.

Formulae for calculating the maximum load a given diameter, extra-flexible galvanised steel wire rope could lift, allowing for a safe working factor of six, had to be memorised. Any calculations had to be made in front of the examiner using the pencil and paper allowed for the purpose.

I rather suspect that my late endeavour to cram as much nautical studying into my time preceding the final exams, led to the dissolution of my short relationship with Wendy.

Besides, when my time at Warsash was over, I would be heading back to sea.

Time spent at sea was always a natural killer of relationships.

I had done my very best.

On this occasion, the issue of a Second Mates Certificate Of Competency was proving elusive.

When I left the School Of Navigation on the 25th of July, I was bitterly disappointed at the final exam results. I had done really well in most subjects but had to accept defeat in others. At least I had gained an enormous amount of knowledge that was absent six months previously.

The British Merchant Navy deck officer was considered an elite among the shipping companies of the world. Without doubt, The Board Of Trade set the highest qualification standards internationally. To obtain that elusive certificate was no longer a dream. It was a goal.

But it would have to wait a little longer.

Back at home, I had five weeks leave accrued. Plans were already being nurtured.

Mark and I decided we would ride our new Hondas to Lands End. from there we would continue to John O' Groats before returning home. We reckoned it would take a week or two.

The day we set off was bright and sunny. Just as well, my only waterproof clothing was a last minute purchase of a Belstaff waxed-cotton jacket. Mark had none but considered his full-face helmet to be adequate wet-weather gear. Everything else was trendy blue denim.

We had glorious weather for the first twenty-four hours. Then it began to rain.

It rained so heavily that we spent an entire day in our two-man tent outside Torquay trying to dry out. Quite a challenge trying to find sufficient amusement in a tiny tent for that length of time.

Anyway, it proved a waste of time as the rain was relentless. So we set off the next day in yet more rain. I suspect Mark was rather envious of my Belstaff. To our credit we arrived at Lands End that evening and erected the tent near the cliff edge.

Another mistake. In addition to the constant rain, the wind strengthened and we spent the entire night taking it in turns to hold onto the ridge pole.

The morning brought a reprieve. The rain had eased to a slight drizzle, so we packed up and moved on.

Being footloose and fancy free, our journey took us along the North Cornish coast and into Wales.

We were still a long way from our intended destination but enjoying the adventure and happy to go where the road was leading us. I managed to find a pair of garish, high visibility fisherman's leggings, but Mark was adamant that his clothing would dry out and be sufficient for the duration.

Then it began raining properly again. Heavily too.

At a cafe on Llanfairpwllgwyngyll railway station platform, on the Island of Anglsey, I looked across at Mark over the steam that was rising from two mugs of tea. Eight days into our adventure and seven of them spent unable to dry out. Intrepid we may have been, fools we were not.

"Are you thinking what I am thinking?" I asked Mark. But he just smiled in resignation.

Ironically, during the last part of our blat down the A5 towards home, the sun began to shine!

Chapter 26

ACT 2

That summer of 1975 passed all too quickly, but was just sufficient for me to spend some quality moments with family and friends.

In addition to time spent with Mark, Bern and Paul, I became involved with a local motorcycle club. This was to be the first of many.

I was duly summoned to Tilbury docks on the 7th of September to join container ship ACT 2.

Being an elder sister to ACT 6, almost everything I have previously described about this class of vessel remains similar. The major obvious difference was that time and weather had taken its toll.

Since launch, ACT 2 had by now more than paid for itself and really deserved a new coat of paint.

Although I was nearing the end of my cadet agreement with Cunard, the personnel department were very supportive and I was retained as Third Mate with a corresponding pay scale. In reality, I was uncertificated at that rank and was only entitled to a cadet's meagre wages.

'Uncert' ranking was not uncommon in the Merchant Navy. In fact, I knew of many third and fourth officers who spent their entire careers at sea whilst remaining uncertificated.

This was to be my last appointment under the terms of my agreement which, if rigidly imposed, could lead to future unemployment with Cunard.

With all this in mind, I set about doing the job I was being paid for, but with a heavy sense of foreboding about the final outcome of my time aboard.

As expected, we sailed from Tilbury for Liverpool to complete discharge and then loading.

I managed to cross The Mersey by ferry to visit my grandmother who lived in Moreton, which I endeavoured to do whenever I was in Liverpool.

From Liverpool, it was an almost straight run out to Melbourne, with just a short stop for bunkers, stores and most importantly, mail, in Cape Town.

Among the mail was a letter from home informing me that Mark had been involved in a serious motorcycle accident. He was in hospital with a shattered arm and leg. Although surgeons pinned his limbs and repaired him to almost new, Mark understandably lost his enthusiasm for bikes.

For three days after leaving South Africa, the sea was extremely rough with a corresponding mountainous swell. The movement of ACT 2 in this type of sea prevented most of us from getting a proper night's sleep. The bunk-beds were arranged in a fore-and-aft direction which meant that falling out of bed became commonplace whenever the ship rolled heavily.

Attempting to counter the problem, I packed surplus lifejackets under the mattress in such a manner that I would spend my sleeping hours squashed up against the adjacent bulkhead.

On this ship I had the fortune to sail with John Brocklehurst, the Second Mate, and his effervescent wife, Denise.

Every once in a while I would meet individuals during my travels with whom it was a pleasure to share time. John and Denise were not only among these, but have remained firm friends to this day. We always exchange Christmas cards and I visit whenever I'm in Warwickshire.

Unlike many other Second Mates, John was always on the bridge in plenty of time to take over the watch from me at midday and midnight. We would invariably share a joke or two and often I would stay and we would talk about nothing in particular until well into his watch.

Spare time was limited, but on this trip I had a Linguaphone German language course on cassette tapes. Fluency was never achieved, but at least I seemed convincing when I explained to listeners that I loved my job as the controller of the Munich tramway system.

During the morning of Wednesday, 15th of October, ACT 2 berthed at the container terminal in Melbourne. Discharge of containers began straight away and discussions were underway to see who, if anyone, would get time to go ashore.

I managed to go into the city by myself for a few hours later that afternoon but can recall it was raining heavily. Interestingly, I was able to avoid some of the weather as I stumbled across a motorcycle exhibition in the centre of town and so stayed until closing time.

By the following afternoon, ACT 2 was ready to leave. After a crew, and possible stowaway check, I reported to the bridge for a three p.m. departure.

We were bound for Wellington in New Zealand and were due to arrive the following Sunday as the passage across the The Tasman Sea would take three-and-a half days.

From the New Zealand coast, it was back across the vast Pacific Ocean to Panama and Tilbury.

Without home leave, I was due for a 'double-header'. This had become standard practice within the company and required all officers and crew to remain with the ship to repeat the previous voyage. All merchant ships only earned money whilst at sea and ACT 2 was a big earner.

The only time I was ever really ill during my ten years at sea occurred during the homeward passage across The Pacific on ACT 2.

During one of my morning watches, I recall having taken a sun sight and began the calculation. The page in my sight book had become unusually blurred and I began to feel dizzy.

I stumbled out onto the bridge wing for fresh air but passed out.

For two full days I had no recollection of events.

The first person I remember seeing when I regained consciousness was Denise. She had maintained a regular vigil at my bedside until I woke.

Denise was able to tell me that I had suffered from an intense fever that had worried the captain. The nearest hospital was in Panama, but Panama was still five day's steaming away.

As usual, there was no doctor on board, and although I slowly made a full recovery, my condition was never diagnosed.

Chapter 27

Summer Of '76

On 27th of February 1976, ACT 2 docked at the container terminal at Tilbury.

I knew I had accrued substantial leave over the past twelve months, but at the time, had no idea that I was not going back to sea for the next five months.

When I arrived home, a heap of mail was waiting for my attention. Among the heap was a large manilla envelope. This envelope contained a copy of my duly completed cadet contract with Cunard together with an employer's reference. It was signed by the head of Fleet Personnel.

Another letter invited me to company head office with an offer of a further contract.

This was the letter that ended my apprehension of the last six months. What a relief!

At last, I did not have to worry any more about my immediate future. Fleet Personnel must have regarded my contribution to the company sufficiently highly to offer me such a contract.

In addition to dealing with head office, I had other pressing commitments that demanded attention before I could settle into leave mode.

Whilst aboard ACT 2, I had applied to take my motorcycle test during my next leave. Of course at the time of application, I could only guess when my leave would start. The motorcycle test centre in Hitchin had written to me with a test date.

In just four day's time!

I hadn't been near a bike for almost six months, and now I had to become proficient in four days!

I wasted no time in prepping the Honda and went out in whatever weather the four days threw at me in order to practice. The Highway Code became bedtime reading and family members were suitably harassed into oral testing.

On the day, the god of two wheels was smiling. I managed to engage the examiner in a short conversation before the test started and slipped in the fact that I had been driving ships until the previous week. I will never know if it affected his judgement, but he passed me anyway.

My leave of 1976 was really beginning to take off. The ride home was a paltry eight miles, but it took me some hours to get there via Cambridgeshire and Essex.

I was happier than Larry. One Sunday in late March, I spent the entire day meticulously cleaning the Honda, right down to the last bolt. Perhaps a premonition was in play.

The very next day I took a ride out to Biggleswade and stopped off at a well-established motorcycle dealer by the name of Bryants. My jaw must have dropped at what I saw.

There, in the window of the main showroom, were the two bikes of my dreams - a Triumph T160 Trident and a Norton Commando Mark 3. Both were being offered at a significant discount.

I was aware that the British motorcycle industry was struggling to compete with foreign imports, but I never expected to see a price reduction on the two most iconic and exciting products they had yet produced.

A salesman quickly spotted my dribbling at the window and invited me inside to extol the virtues and specifications of both machines. He needn't have bothered. I had 'read the print off' every road test article that had featured these bikes in the previous year's motorcycle press.

They would have to remain a dream. Even with the discount, I just couldn't afford the upgrade.

Our salesman was obviously having a slack day and insisted on number crunching based on my meagre funds and the part-exchange value of my Honda.

Somehow he managed to manipulate figures and included a ridiculously generous offer on my immaculate Honda. All of a sudden I could afford a brand new Norton Commando Mark 3!

Although the Trident was a fabulous-looking bike, the Norton won the day due to it having a twin cylinder engine as opposed to the Trident's three cylinders. The benefit to me was simple, I could service the Norton more easily by myself.

Paperwork was completed without too much protest from me, even though I handed over the last five pounds in cash I had to my name. My bank account was drained and my wallet empty.

But that didn't matter a jot. I had now entered the realm of the super-bike.

Having to wait two whole days before the bike could be collected was agonising, but on the 26th of March, I roared away from Bryants imagining everyone I passed was staring with envy.

Straight round to Mark's house, and when he saw the gleaming Norton parked outside, I was subject to all sorts of expletives. Mark had recovered from his motorcycle accident but never followed my lead on this occasion by acquiring a similar motorbike. Rather sad, really.

Being totally broke until my next pay day meant that socialising involving expenditure was on hold. However, an invitation to a private party in Welwyn Garden City was within my price range.

It was at this gathering that I met Angela Leyton. She was a bubbly character and we talked well into the night. In fact, it had become so late that I was invited to stay over by Angela's sister Sue, who was the party host. A refusal may have offended, so I agreed.

Although no commitments were made to keep in touch, Angela tracked me down later that week to Bern's house which was a mere stone's throw from hers. Bern and I were working on an old motorbike when Angela appeared. I looked at Bern but he just smiled. This was no coincidence.

Angela and I formed a partnership from that day onwards, and she became my pillion passenger whenever there was a chance of a ride out or party. Most other evenings we would meet up at The Holly Bush pub in Welwyn Garden City which was local to where she and Bern lived.

Life had improved dramatically for me since beginning my leave in late February.

I had a secure job, a fun-loving and loyal girlfriend, I had passed my motorcycle test and was the proud owner of one of the most respectable motorcycles of its era.

To cap it all, we were heading into one of the best summers on record.

Yes, the summer of 1976 was set to become truly memorable.

Wheels, 1976

Chapter 28

All Good Things

The long, hot summer of 1976 was, without doubt, the best I can remember.

The fledgling motorcycle club was attracting new members, and our regular meetings at the Lemsford Cafe became a hotspot for ideas. Over sausage sandwiches and hot tea, and while listening to the latest chart-toppers on the juke box, plans were discussed for ride-outs.

One balmy night, I suggested to the group at the cafe that as it was so pleasant outside, maybe we should take the opportunity to see where the road could take us. The others readily agreed.

The road that night took us to Swanage on the south coast.

Without any sleep, we still had mini adventures the next day in and around that town, which culminated in a rock and roll competition with another motorcycle club from Guildford.

Over the following weeks, Bern had parties, Mark had parties, and unknown to my parents, I had parties. During a rare quiet moment, Dave Halliday, a club member, expressed his envy at my choice of career. Although we were both the same age, he felt his life was going nowhere and that the club had become his family.

This was rather sad news to hear at the time, but became tragically poignant when Dave was killed in a motorcycle accident while riding his new Honda CB 750 a few weeks later.

He was given a full biker's funeral.

Around this time, I asked Angela if she would like to join me for a short holiday in Blackpool. She didn't need asking twice. But there was a problem. Understandably, Angela's parents did not initially approve of the idea, especially as they didn't yet know me very well, and the journey would be by motorcycle. However, Angela finally won them over. I later learned that suggestions had been made that one day they may have a ship's captain as a son-in-law!

The holiday in Blackpool went ahead and was followed by numerous ride-outs to interesting destinations.

By this time I had joined The Norton Owner's Club and Angela accompanied me to our first rally at Olney in Buckinghamshire. The local pub, The Two Brewers, provided food, beer and entertainment, whilst back at the campsite we added all sorts of games. These included an egg and spoon race where the holder of the spoon sat rearward on the pillion seat of a motorcycle during an all out race across a field to a finish line. Not many eggs survived and the field was littered with pillion passengers who failed to hang on sufficiently.

Our local motorcycle club had grown to about two dozen regular members and evening destinations often included a pub. On a visit to The Pyramid pub in Stevenage one evening, we were escorted by two police cars which remained in the pub car park until satisfied there was unlikely to be trouble. These were days when motorcycle groups were associated with violence.

This view was sometimes justified. At a rock concert in Hertford one evening, our group caught the attention of a large group of 'mods' who must have rated their chances. Without warning, they began throwing punches which were naturally reciprocated. Fortunately, we had some very handy members within our group so managed to hold our own until police arrived. Surprisingly, there were no serious injuries to our group, and the police response was to see us off the premises with no further repercussions.

August arrived without warning and my leave days were evaporating fast. The entire summer had been a whirlwind of adventures but now I had to face the reality of leaving it all behind to begin earning again. Reluctantly, I resigned myself to the fact that all good things must come to an end.

Saying goodbye to Angela without knowing when I would come home again was particularly hard.

On August the 8th, I flew from Heathrow to Houston in Texas with some other replacement officers for my next appointment. This was to be a Brocklebank tramp ship. I was happy. Tramp ships could be fun.

On arrival at Houston, we discovered that our ship, the motor vessel 'Maihar' was berthed in New Orleans, suggesting that someone at head office was responsible for a major blunder. To add to the chaos, we were housed for the night in a dilapidated motel outside Houston airport with cockroaches as bed pals. Most of the ship's relief spent the entire night in a local bar.

The following day we made the connecting flight to New Orleans. I had been there before as a cadet on Manipur four years previously and found it to be an exciting city. However, loading was already in progress and the officers due to leave were eager to get away.

Although a tramp, Maihar was a fine looking ship. She was built for the East India trade and her crew were from that sub-continent. Moored against the quayside in the summer sunshine, Maihar looked resplendent in tropical white with red boot-topping. Her company colours of blue and white had been freshly painted as bands on the black funnel. All the officers were British and she was to be commanded from now on by Captain Pembridge.

Maihar sailed from New Orleans with a general cargo for South American ports along the coast of Peru. Talara and Salaverry were our first discharge ports but were little more than crumbling concrete wharves with no shoreside entertainment whatsoever. Up to this time, I had believed all South America was the land of eternal fiesta. Disappointment. Peru was stuck in The Third World.

Callao was different. Being Peru's largest port, bright lights could be seen on our approach. Lima, the capital, was only eight miles inland so hopes were high.

Our third engineer, Jimmy Tipton, was a native of North Wales and we shared a similar outlook on life. One afternoon, we were given shore leave and so took a bus into the capital at a cost of seven soles, the Peruvian currency of the time. There were sixty-five soles to a U.S. dollar, so travel, like everything else in Peru, was incredibly cheap.

Jimmy and I walked for miles around Lima and were surprised at the large numbers of armed police and military personnel everywhere we ventured. Peru was a dictatorship - and it showed.

Outside a cafe in one of the many squares, Jimmy and I met up with our radio operator and two other engineers from Maihar. They had paid a taxi driver six hundred soles each for their eight mile journey. Realising they had been fleeced, they agreed to return by bus.

The evening was still relatively young when Jimmy and I returned to Callao so we decided to stop off at one of the numerous seedy bars that littered the dockland.

Music was being played and the bar was full of foreign seamen and local women. It became quite obvious that trade between the two was brisk. Jimmy and I had several cold beers and settled into watching the nightlife and fending off several offers from the senoritas. Bus rates didn't apply here, and besides, we had been warned about some of the consequences.

Suddenly, two military trucks screeched to a halt outside the bar. A powerful searchlight pierced the windows and the clientele within ran for rear doors and any point of escape.

A dozen soldiers brandishing machine guns stormed into the bar to find only Jimmy and I still sat on our bar stools. We were both roughly pushed up against a back wall and searched. Both of us had our issue Board Of Trade Seaman's cards with us and these were taken by the officer in charge.

Jimmy and I were handcuffed and taken to a police station where we spent a miserable and extremely apprehensive night in a cold concrete cell.

At that time, we had no idea that we had breached Callao's strict curfew laws.

Chapter 29

Phantom Fiestas

One night in a cold concrete cell. It was sobering. There was no ventilation, furnishing of any kind, and it stank like nothing I had experienced before. No doubt due to the drain hole in one corner which served as a toilet. Jimmy and I were worried. Very worried. I had read books about such places and was aware that in a dictatorship, people just sometimes disappeared.

Only a few short weeks ago, I was revelling in the best summer I had ever experienced. It was still only August of 1976 and now I was experiencing another extreme. This was bleak.

The heavy steel door opened and two uniformed men, one with a machine-gun, entered the cell. The other man was wearing dark sunglasses and had several medals pinned to his tunic.

It was this man who spoke in very poor English "So, I theenk you learn important lesson, no?"

Jimmy and I looked at each other and nodded vigorously.

"You now know about midnight curfew, yes?"

More vigorous nodding. I was about to point out that the police raid last night was actually fifteen minutes early, but thought better of it.

The man with the sunglasses threw our seaman's cards onto the dirty cell floor and left. Jimmy and I picked them up inquisitively. The man with the gun pushed us into a corridor and then out onto the street where the sun was already high in the sky. Was that it? Were we free?

The walk back to our ship was one of immense relief. However, having covered some distance, it dawned on me that the cash that had been taken from us by the police the night before had not been returned. Should we go back? The decision was instantaneous. We carried on.

Back on board the safety of Maihar, I had to explain my overnight absence to the chief officer. Sympathetically, he laughed at the misadventure, but was also unaware of the curfew. The news spread like wildfire around the ship and no other crewman suffered the same indignation.

Receiving mail from home (or anywhere else for that matter) was always eagerly anticipated. For some reason, very little had yet arrived and morale suffered as a result. I considered myself fortunate to be the recipient of two whole letters from the U.K. Both of them had been written by a girl I had only just met before leaving home. Although very pleased, I was intrigued as to how she had obtained a forwarding address and managed to have her letters by-pass the inevitable pile of other mail that must have been waiting for us. Her name was Kim Williams.

Materani, a small Peruvian port close to the border with Chile was our next destination. Our bulk cargo of American-aid wheat was finally discharged here and we were only too happy to cast off and make for another port. The fiestas we had hoped for never materialised and I was soon to learn that all the fun to be had in South America generally took place on the east coast of the continent.

Leaving Materani, I was stationed on the afterdeck to supervise the letting go of our heavy polypropylene mooring ropes. This completed, I also let go of the line to the tug that had eased the ship off the quay. We were now under our own power and manoeuvring towards the harbour entrance.

Maihar was fitted with a single, variable-pitch propeller, which enabled her to move forwards or backwards depending on the angle of the propeller blades.

To complete our manoeuvre, the blades were set to run astern to allow the bow to swing to port.

Nothing happened. The propeller was still turning but the blades refused to budge. We were now surging ahead towards a rocky cliff line. Captain Pembridge ordered the engine stopped and the anchor dropped. Carnage ensued. The bow of Maihar, en route to an inevitable beaching, had first to plough through numerous local fishing boats that had been attached to buoys.

I raced to the port side of the ship just in time to witness the port anchor plummet into a fishing boat that had been caught under the flare of our bow. The boat splintered into hundreds of pieces of flying wood. Amazingly, some of the fishing boat crews were still aboard their craft. But not for long. I watched as these unfortunates dived for their lives into the harbour waters.

The port anchor release was quickly followed by the starboard anchor and all headway was checked before we hit the rocks ahead. Very fortunate. Damage to Maihar was minimal and no one aboard wanted to spend time effecting repairs in such a desolate port.

As for the fishermen, I never heard any more. I believe there were no serious injuries and suppose some form of compensation must have been offered.

This whole incident understandably shook Captain Pembridge and we stayed in Materani only long enough to overhaul and test the variable-pitch mechanism.

Our last port on the Peruvian coast was Pisco. Quite a large town but as bleak and austere as all the others. Here we loaded fish-meal. This was dry, ground fish bones that was intended as a fertiliser. Filthy, smelly stuff. All the exposed pipework in the hatches had to be sealed, including the carbon dioxide fire smothering system. Dust from the loading tubes found its way into every nook and cranny aboard and the smell permeated everything. This was tramp shipping at its worst, but at least we now knew we were to return to the U.S.A. and morale began to improve.

Once Maihar was clear of Pisco, the entire ship was washed down. Cabins were cleaned and our passage along the west coast of South America towards The Panama Canal passed under blue skies and through calm tropical sea. Maybe there would be mail waiting for us in Panama?

I have never returned to Peru. I have never regretted it.

Chapter 30

Tugboat Tony

On about the 10th of October 1976, Maihar arrived at Gulfport, Mississippi.

I was at my berthing station at the after end of the ship as a tugboat came alongside to assist us in manoeuvring. The tugboat skipper was interested in where we had come from and soon we were engaged in a conversation whilst handling mooring ropes and winches. This served as an indication of the easy attitude taken to life by the amiable Americans of the southern states.

When safely alongside the quay, I asked the tugboat crew if they knew of any motorcycle dealerships in the area. In answering, the skipper said that as soon as I could get ashore, he would pick me up in his truck and take me to visit the local motorcycle emporium.

As luck would have it, no cargo was to be discharged that day, so I became the first member of the ship's complement to benefit from a guided tour of Gulfport and the surrounding countryside.

The tugboat skipper, whose name I have now sadly forgotten, was accompanied on the tour by his crew. His crew's name was Tony. They were a two-man team.

For an entire afternoon and evening, I was shown all that was worth seeing in Gulfport. The motorcycle dealership was, not unsurprisingly, part of the Harley-Davidson franchise and was stocked with all manner of appealing bikes and Harley merchandise. On leaving, my mind was racing: One day, maybe?

I couldn't help but notice the shotgun that was clipped to the dashboard of the skipper's truck. The explanation I was given for its inclusion left me in no doubt that Misssissippi, like the other American states, had a crime rate that frequently involved guns.

The evening ended with a visit to an out-of-town roadhouse. There was a large bar area and a jukebox to one side. It must have been a popular venue as it was packed with locals. I can clearly recall the sound of Deep Purple's 'Smoke On The Water' blasting out from the jukebox as the three of us entered. A uniformed and armed guard stood by the door which added to my curiosity about this part of the world. Bottled beers were quickly produced and the evening developed into an interesting mix of loud rock music and even louder discussions involving the different cultures between the U.S.A. and the U.K.

Tony, in particular, seemed fascinated about anything connected with the U.K., and I had trouble trying to pay for any of the rounds of beer. He was obviously interested in the rock scene and when I mentioned a few of my favourites, they mysteriously formed part of the jukebox's playlist.

Before leaving the roadhouse much later that evening - or morning - I can't quite remember, I had acquired a number of new friends from Gulfport who insisted I return whenever I could. Additionally, I came away with a souvenir magnum revolver cartridge from the security guard as I had shown a passing interest in the handgun he was carrying. What friendly people!

I kept that cartridge right up until the time I joined Hertfordshire Police. For obvious reasons I lawfully, but somewhat regretfully, disposed of it.

That following day, I had to be out on deck early to open up the cargo holds that were to be worked. As the heavy steel sections of the MacGregor hatch over number two cargo space were slowly sliding open, the sight that greeted me was one of horror!

We had loaded hundreds of tons of powdered fishmeal into the space I was staring into. What I saw was a writhing white sea. I looked closer. Maggots! Millions of them!

I summoned the chief officer who was equally baffled at the horrific sight. The hatch cover was closed. Further enquiries with ship's agent and importer confirmed that the phenomena was not uncommon and that it took only a hint of moisture to cause the transformation. Forming a more positive view, we were told that the maggots should only be a few inches deep near the surface!

Number two hatch was reopened and soon afterwards, huge crane-mounted grabs were taking massive bites of fishmeal and maggots from the surface of the cargo and loading it onto railway wagons that were waiting on the quayside. Fishmeal dust escaped from the mechanical grabs and clouds of the stuff settled on the ship's deck and quayside.

Further hatches were opened and the same sight repeated. At the end of that first working day, it was necessary to sweep the hatch side rails clear of the dust. As no cadets were aboard Maihar, that duty fell to me.

With one hatch left to go (the only one that hadn't yet been touched), I was feeling buoyant at the prospect of another evening ashore, when my footing slipped on the hatch rail. My right leg plunged into the cargo, quickly followed by the rest of my terrified carcass. The 'inch-or-so' of writhing maggots turned out to be a 'foot-or-so'. I managed to hook the broom I had been using over the hatch coaming and pull myself to a place where I was able to climb out. I was covered in stinking fishmeal and maggots. I had maggots in my boots, inside my boiler suit, all my pockets and I even spat out a couple the little creatures onto the deck.

My shower that evening took a little longer than usual and my ordeal that day had provided some amusement to the rest of the crew.

By the time I reached the dock gates, Tony was waiting as arranged and sitting behind the wheel of a Chevrolet pickup that would have a British MOT examiner rubbing his hands.

Another evening spent in and around Gulfport has left me with many warm memories. The tugboat skipper made only infrequent appearances during my stay in the port, but Tony informed me that his skipper was not as well as he would have me believe, so we hit the town without him.

When Tony had first asked me which rock bands I currently rated, I had included AC/DC and Hawkwind. En route to yet another roadhouse, we listened to tracks from these bands as Tony had made a point of obtaining copies on cassette that very day from a Gulfport record store.

When I described my swimming lesson with the maggots, Tony couldn't stop laughing and on arrival at our destination he went out of his way to tell everyone he knew at the roadhouse - which turned out to be everyone!

Again, I was warmly welcomed by all the customers Tony introduced me to - including a couple of his girlfriends who kept me repeating certain sentences so they could wonder at my accent.

I was getting very little sleep during our stay in Gulfport due to the late nights and early mornings but it was all well worth it. Each evening when I was finished for the day, I would meet up with Tony and set off on another venture. Walking along the quayside toward the dock gates, I slowly became accustomed to the crunching underfoot of maggots that had evolved from the dust and now covered every surface in Maihar's vicinity.

Eventually, it was time to leave this port and all the memories that had been created.

Tony insisted that we keep up a correspondence, so home addresses were exchanged and promises made to forward photographs and endeavour to visit again if ever in the vicinity.

As Maihar cast off her lines to Tony's tug and made her way slowly into the buoyed channel leading out to the open sea, there was furious waving between vessels and the last I ever saw of Tugboat Tony was when he was standing in the tug's bow holding a camera.

Some months later I received a letter from Tony with a photograph of Maihar leaving Gulfport. He had written a rather poignant message on the reverse. I still have the photograph, and although we corresponded several times, this was another case of 'goodbye' meaning just that.

Chapter 31

Gremlins

Maihar left Gulfport in ballast. This term refers to a merchant ship that is empty of any cargo. In order to maintain stability and ensure the propeller remains submerged, sufficient sea water is pumped into the double-bottom tanks. This weight is known as ballast.

From a photograph taken of Maihar as she left Gulfport, it is clear that the ship had a pronounced starboard list. When our engineers tried to correct the list, it became apparent that transfer valves were faulty and would need repair.

So in this unsatisfactory condition, Maihar edged her way through the Gulf Of Mexico, around the southern coast of Florida and north-east along the eastern seaboard of The U.S.A.

We were heading for Canada.

While the engineers were struggling with faulty valves, our carpenter was struggling with blocked toilets in the engineer's changing room. Just before lunchtime on a fairly calm day, I had joined others in the officer's bar for a beer or two. The bar, engineer's changing room and engineer's accommodation, were all on the same deck and in quite close proximity. Our second engineer, a rather short, rotund and balding man in his late forties, entered the bar. Still dressed in a boiler suit, he was keen to join our group and intimated that he would be with us as soon as he had changed.

The convivial atmosphere of the bar that lunchtime was suddenly disrupted by a terrifically loud hissing sound emanating from the engineer's changing room across the corridor. This was followed in quick succession by a series of screams from our second engineer's cabin. The bar emptied as all souls raced to the location of the screaming.

We found our second engineer standing naked - except for his slippers and spectacles - in the doorway of his en-suite shower room. The inside of the shower room was coated in a stinking, dark green substance that matched that on our engineer. When he removed his spectacles, the two rings around his eyes seemed the only part of his body that had escaped his ordeal.

In addition to the mess in the shower room, there was a neat stripe of green slime running down the wall of his cabin exactly opposite to the open doorway that he was standing in.

The cause of all the mayhem was attributed to our carpenter who had decided to try a high-pressure airline to unblock the adjacent toilets. Problem solved!

Although it took hours of volunteer work to make the second engineer's cabin reasonably habitable again, the smell lingered for weeks. Of course, he had our deep sympathy, but the sight of him standing in his shower doorway provided raucous laughter in the bar for even longer.

Our destination was to be Hamilton, on the western shore of Lake Ontario. This necessitated a long passage of the Saint Lawrence Seaway. Captain Pembridge was still anxious about the stability of Maihar due to the faulty transfer valves but was no doubt relieved when we collected a pilot on the approach to Quebec.

I was engaged on extended bridge watches during the entire passage of the Saint Lawrence since weather conditions were unfavourable and shipping density increased considerably as the waterway narrowed. We encountered patches of dense fog which caused us to slow down to a speed that only just maintained steerage, and navigation was by radar alone.

Air temperature was well below freezing, which was quite normal for this part of the world in November, and served to remind me of a previous experience in Russia.

A series of locks had to be negotiated to allow for the tidal patterns which were extreme.

On our approach to the first set of locks, all appeared well as the fog had cleared and visibility was good. Even the variable-pitch propeller was performing faultlessly.

Maihar was on an even keel and Captain Pembridge appeared satisfied with his ship's progress.

We were now heading perfectly towards the centre of the open lock entrance and were only metres away when Maihar slowly rolled to starboard. There was no time to take evasive action and with an almighty crash, our starboard accommodation superstructure hit the massively strong concrete side wall of the first piece of Canada that we had encountered.

Captain Pembridge was horrified as his ship came to an abrupt halt. The pilot just stared forward in disbelief. I stared at both of them feeling relief at being just a junior officer.

Tugs extricated Maihar and assisted while we moored to a convenient quayside. There was to be no more movement until the valves were made serviceable once and for all!

For the next two days, Canadian engineers worked alongside our engineers to replace any faulty valves they discovered.

The real victim of our collision with the lock wall was none other than our second engineer. His cabin, although now clean and odourless, had taken the full impact of the mishap, and as a result, had been crushed inwards like an aluminium can. Repairs were effected but his two windows were replaced by heavy steel plates which excluded any natural light, and his walls (bulkheads) were plain steel as all the formica panelling had to be removed.

We all agreed that Captain Pembridge, who took overall responsibility for his ship, and the second engineer were the unluckiest men aboard.

Would the gremlins now disembark?

Chapter 32

Top Tramp

The middle of November 1976 found Maihar securely moored against a quayside in Hamilton, Ontario. Faulty transfer valves had been replaced and the ship once again considered seaworthy.

Cargo was being loaded for the Middle East, but as luck would have it, the Canadian dockers didn't work weekends. In fact, there were a number of weekdays when there was no cargo work at all due to industrial activity. This provided ample opportunity for travel and sightseeing, even though it remained bitterly cold for the duration of our stay.

Niagara Falls was only an hour away by road. I took a bus there with a couple of others from the ship but found the whole experience disappointing. I was expecting too much. Instead of being awe-struck as no doubt early explorers would have been, I felt like the average tourist that I had become.

As bus passengers, we were shepherded by a guide through crowds of even more tourists who were all trying to get photographs of the brink of the falls without other people cluttering the frame. Why not just settle for a postcard?

I did. Anyway, fancy ruining a world wonder by building a town with all its tourist trappings adjacent to such a magnificent waterfall.

At the weekend I hired a car and took three of my shipmates to explore Toronto. Always a gamble when others are involved. Previous experience had taught me that a seafarer will normally head to the nearest bar regardless of local attractions. So Jimmy Tipton and I left two of our small group in a nearby bar while we set off in the hire car to see as much of the city as we had time for.

There were plenty of bars in Hamilton and they were frequently visited by Jimmy and me when work had finished for the day. Labatts beer seemed omnipresent and although drinkable, both of us agreed that we wouldn't be sorry if we never saw that label again.

Back at the ship, our chief steward had negotiated a deal with the chandler to take aboard sufficient Labatts beer to last for the following three months!

On the 24th of November, Maihar left Hamilton bound for New York.

The passage to The Big Apple was quite challenging from a navigational point of view. Frequent dense fog coupled with short, overcast days meant that accurate position fixing was impossible. Dead-reckoning and radar images of the coastline were our only aids.

Nevertheless, we arrived safely at a berth in Brooklyn, in the shadow of the famous bridge, and began taking aboard assorted dry cargo.

Here was further evidence in my mind that tramp ships were top of the fleet in creating opportunity for adventure. Maihar had her mechanical faults, and with the starboard side accommodation looking as if we had returned from a war zone, she was not at her best. But no member of her crew could become weary at the variety of ports we visited.

At the very first opportunity, I took a bus into Manhattan. I was alone this time and was free to wander wherever I liked. The World Trade Centre building was on my list and it was a truly weird sensation, looking up at one of the twin towers from ground level. I bought a ticket to the observation deck and experienced an express lift for the first time. I still have a photograph of Manhattan taken from the top of the tower and even kept the ticket as a souvenir.

Wandering around that great metropolis alone, trying out the Metro and queuing for a hamburger without understanding the meaning of 'all the way', has left me with memories for life.

Before we sailed, members of Brooklyn's 'Merchant Navy Comforts Association' visited the ship and left a wrapped Christmas present for each member of the crew.

My Christmas box contained a knitted wool hat, a pair of warm socks, writing paper, a pen and several 'candy bars' - all of which were put to good use before the big day itself, which was still two weeks distant. Yet more wonderful people. It would never happen on QE2.

Maihar left Brooklyn for the Middle East with a full cargo of North American exports.

On the big day itself, we arrived at Port Said in time to transit the Suez Canal. Due to the expected chaos of forming into transit convoys, our Christmas celebrations were re-scheduled for the 28th of December.

On that day, whilst cruising down the Red Sea, Christmas lunch was enjoyed by all the officers not on watch. Luckily, that included me.

The turkey that was provided by the chief steward was washed down with copious quantities from his vast stock of Labatts beer.

Speculation was rife that our chief steward had made a significant backhander from the deal with the chandler.

Khorramshah is a small Iranian port on the east bank of the Shatt-Al-Arab River which is a natural border between Iran and Iraq. It was here that our cargo was discharged. Because of tensions between the two neighbours, there were soldiers of both armies clearly visible. Gunboats regularly cruised past Maihar with crews ominously pointing weapons at any human movement. There was no possibility of shore leave!

A decision had been made by Cunard that Maihar would sail to Singapore for repairs. She certainly needed them as she visually looked as if she was falling apart. There were also rumours that she may be sold, so needed to appear in a saleworthy condition.

We arrived at Sembawang Shipyard in Singapore on the 3rd of February 1977. Sembawang was situated on the Johore Strait, at the very northern tip of Singapore Island, eleven miles from Singapore City in the south.

The crossing of the Indian Ocean had been uncomfortable due to the fact that most of the crew, including myself, had suffered severe colds with 'flu-like symptoms for most of the passage. There was no possibility of taking a day off sick so our watch routines continued as normal.

Torrential rain delivered by the north-east monsoon prevented much activity while we waited to dry-dock. So once again, taxis were summoned and Jimmy and I would journey into Singapore City for some rest and recreation. Sitting comfortably in the billiard room of Raffles hotel, sipping gin and fresh limes was a particularly pleasant pastime.

I had been with Maihar now for a full six months, and as we had no one aboard that we could trust with a pair of scissors, most of the crew, including Captain Pembridge and myself, had grown long hair and full-sets. It was time to find a barber.

Suitably groomed and refreshed, Jimmy and I returned late to the ship at Sembawang.

For the next three weeks, there was very little work for the deck officers, so our time was put to recreational use. Between trips to the city, Jimmy and I created our own entertainment on board. This included impromptu rock concerts in the bar as we now had a decent sound system and new cassettes to play. These were quite popular with the younger officers and we even managed to make a dent in the mountain of Labatts.

When I was notified near the end of the month that I would be flying home on the 28th, I was both elated and saddened at the same time.

Maihar had been a good ship with a happy crew, many of whom I considered friends, but knew I was unlikely to ever see again. We had experienced many cultures, had memorable incidents both good and bad, and lots of adventures along the way.

Maihar was certainly a 'Top Tramp'.

Chapter 33

An Old Friend

On the 17th of November 1977, having flown out to Holland, I joined Port Nicholson in Antwerp.

This ship was very familiar to me as I had spent four months on her three years previously. Most of the crew were being changed and I had got to know several of the new faces as we had flown out as a group.

During the summer of that year, it became apparent that there were fewer vacancies becoming available within Cunard's fleet, and I had enjoyed an unprecedented nine months at home. This time however, it hadn't been all fun and adventure. I had made a serious attempt at studying in my own time with a view to sit and pass the almost insurmountable second mate's examination.

At the time of leaving home, I knew I had passed the dreaded oral exam, but now had to wait for the results of the written exams. I was on a knife edge.

The once proud Port Nicholson sailed from Antwerp in ballast for Saint John, New Brunswick, in Canada. A ship in ballast earns nothing for its owners and we knew our cargo was to be potatoes for North Africa. This was an indication of the changing fortunes of the shipping industry. One of the finest refrigerated cargo liners ever launched was being relegated to a tramp!

Crossing the North Atlantic at this time of year is rarely a pleasant experience, and a ship in ballast will always suffer more in heavy seas than one that is fully laden. As a result, we really suffered with the constant corkscrew motion, and all on board were relieved when we reached Saint John. I had learned from past experience to be prepared for cold weather, and every stitch of warm clothing was needed out on deck.

Almost immediately, we began loading potatoes. Ironically, the outside air temperature was far lower than our refrigerated cargo spaces. Our charges needed a temperature no lower than three degrees centigrade, otherwise they start to rot. When the outside air temperature fell to freezing point, all cargo work stopped and the hatches secured. It also began snowing. Heavily.

We were now playing nursemaid to two thousand tons of spuds. We had to wait for an improvement in weather before we could load our next quota of four-and-a-half thousand tons.

On the 6th of December, I woke to find I could not see out of my cabin windows because of the hard, thick ice that was coating the glass. The temperature had fallen to minus fifteen degrees and the captain was visited by Canadian authorities who advised that no crew should venture on deck unless fully covered. Any exposed flesh would suffer frost-bite due to an added wind-chill factor.

So when I went ashore later that day, a balaclava, wool hat, scarf and sunglasses were essential items to complete my ensemble. Fortunately, there was hardly anyone outside to notice my appearance, and the walk into town was quite eerie.

I had taken advantage of the stoppage of work to explore what I could in Saint John. Most shops, bars and cafes were open, but there were only a few signs of customers. When I had a conversation with staff in a cafe that I had sought refuge in, they all agreed I must be mad to be out walking in the prevailing conditions. I must admit, it was cold. Very cold. Especially as there was a cutting, icy wind. I opted to take a taxi for my return journey.

Mail from home arrived and I learned that I had passed all the written exams bar one! For that, the Board Of Trade had granted me a referral. So close! Although disappointed at this result, it did mean that I was only a whisker away from a second mate's ticket. All I needed was to get back home at the first opportunity and blitz that one final exam!

After a further two days in which the ship's heating system struggled to cope, the outside temperature rose sufficiently to continue loading. I did get other chances to visit the town and managed to take a series of photographs. I believe Saint John is unique in having the world's only reverse waterfall. It is caused by a natural bar across a river bed which endures tidal flow in both directions. Another one to cross off the list! The loading continued but due to the unpredictable weather, it was painfully slow.

So slow in fact, that we were still alongside on Christmas day which was fully appreciated by the entire ship's complement.

Port Nicholson finally departed Saint John on the last day of the year bound for Algeria. She was down to her marks with six-and-a-half thousand tons of finest Canadian spuds in her holds.

At seventeen knots, we made good speed during the Atlantic crossing and on the 7th of January 1978, the 'Nick' passed through the Straits of Gibraltar. Annaba, on the Algerian coast was awaiting our arrival, but when we dropped anchor off the port on the 8th, we learned that we were just one of twenty merchant ships waiting to go alongside.

After four days of anchor watches, it was our turn to enter the port and begin unloading. The second mate and I split the deck watches which covered each twenty-four hours. It was a routine which didn't leave a lot of time for sight-seeing. I did manage to explore the old Roman part of the town during a Sabbath day, but didn't feel inclined to return.

Annaba was followed by further discharge at Algiers and Mostaganem, so we spent an inordinate amount of time on the North African coast. The Arab workers were incredibly slow and rumours that we were departing for Glasgow were all that kept crew morale from plummeting.

The rumours were crushed in mid-February when we learned that we had been re-routed to South Africa. So on the 20th of February, Port Nicholson finally departed the extreme north of the continent bound for the extreme south.

Cape Town came as a breath of fresh air by comparison, and soon we began loading some of the tastiest apples and pears I had ever encountered.

On the first Sunday in port, I was rostered as duty officer and so had to remain aboard whilst others went ashore. While leaning on the ship's rail close to the gangway, I noticed a man and woman walking along the quayside in my direction. It had begun to rain and the man called up to me and asked if he and his wife could come aboard to shelter until the shower passed over.

I agreed, and a conversation revealed that they were on holiday from England. I asked in which part of England they lived and the reply came "a tiny hamlet you will never have heard of called Little Almshoe in Hertfordshire".

"Actually, I know it well" I replied. " I live in Knebworth, just six miles away".

The next couple of hours was spent in our bar and lounge swapping stories, and long after the rain had stopped I was invited by Mr and Mrs Graham to tea at the Nelson Hotel where they were staying.

The Nelson was the most expensive hotel in Cape Town and I took full advantage of the offer at my first opportunity.

Later that year, I visited the Grahams at their massive, rambling home in Little Almshoe. 'The Wyck' as the house was named, was set in several acres of manicured gardens with tennis courts and stables. I was impressed.

However, I'm not so sure the Grahams felt the same when I turned up on my noisy Norton dressed in black leather and jeans!

Chapter 34

Triumph

On the 18th of March 1978, 'Port Nicholson' was alongside in Port Elizabeth, South Africa, being loaded to her gunnels with Cape fruit.

According to Alan Rattray, our chief officer, I had earned a day off. Very generous, I thought, but the coastal had been hard work for me and the second mate so far. A break was overdue.

Anyway, it was my 24th birthday.

The sun was shining and I spent most of the day on the beach, accompanied by Ken, our radio officer and Jerry, our cadet. I took advantage of the warm sea water by swimming out as far as I dare from the beach, and in the late afternoon our small group indulged in an expensive restaurant meal. Part of the evening included entertainment in a local cinema which was screening the recently released film 'Jaws'. The other part of the evening involved the inevitable bar crawl back to the ship.

As a rule, I seldom suffer from the effects of alcohol, but on this occasion I was conveyed back to Port Nicholson by taxi, having passed out on a grassy central reservation between the two lanes of the coastal highway.

Next morning I was back out on deck with an unbearable hangover. Ken came out to me - his face was as white as mine felt. "It's just been on the news!" he blurted.

"What has?" I rather distantly queried.

"Sharks! Massive ones! Several were seen yesterday in the shallows where you were swimming!"

It was time for a cup of tea in the deck office. Here, Alan, Ken and Jerry added their opinions on the dangers of swimming in shark-infested waters. It had been a birthday I shall not forget.

The return passage to Europe was pleasant but uneventful. Since the 'Nick' was registered as a passenger cargo liner, our quota of twelve examples of human cargo accompanied us.

On the 13th of April, after five months aboard Port Nicholson, I left the ship on arrival in Sheerness. Having served on this magnificent vessel twice, I felt a twinge of sadness as I took a last look at her in the rear-view mirror of my hire car. Eighteen months later, she ended her days at a breaker's yard in China.

My leave was interrupted by visits to the Southampton School of Navigation where I had been enrolled on a number of courses. In May, I gained my 'First Aid At Sea Certificate'. In June, I qualified for a 'Certificate Of Competence In Radiotelephony' held at Southampton University.

In September, I travelled to the Board of Trade buildings in London where I sat my one exam referral for a second mate's certificate. I had studied every possible combination of questions during my leave and practised time and again the calculations required in astronomical navigation.

Apprehension would be an understatement, but after the first half dozen calculations, a quiet confidence emerged and I left the exam room feeling unusually calm. In fact, I was rather surprised when I overheard several of the candidates who had just sat the same exam discussing how tough the questions had been. Complacency can be disastrous.

In early October, an official-looking letter fell on the doormat. I could tell it was from the Board of Trade by the franking marks. I held that letter for some minutes before I could summon the courage to open it. When I did, I felt like I had just won the football pools! Not only had I passed the final exam, but my 'Certificate Of Competency As Second Mate' could be collected in person at any time from the 9th of the month.

So, on the 9th of October, I took a morning train to London and collected what I consider to be the most important document of my lifetime. From my perspective at that time, and having such huge respect for the deck officers of the merchant navy, this was truly a personal triumph.

On the 17th of October, I flew out to Antwerp to join the Brocklebank ship, Markhor.

No letters or documents survive detailing my time on this particular ship, but I have a number of photographs that help stir my memory. I also have a list of officers from the Christmas menu.

Markhor was a tramp ship built for trade in the Far and Middle East, and my next three months were spent tramping around that part of the world. We visited many of the ports that were already familiar to me and as usual, I took every possible opportunity to travel ashore.

The most outstanding memory of that voyage was the calibre of the officers, many of whom became firm friends.

Captain Watkins was a real gentleman who had been the master of the Manipur, the ship in which I first went to sea as a first-trip cadet back in 1972. The second mate, John Cook and his wife, Muriel, shared the cabin next to mine and I was constantly being invited for 'drinks' whenever I was off-watch. For years until John's death, I would visit them at their home in Warsash, where we would exchange stories about our travels.

Our second electrician was Keith Jarrett. A young Yorkshireman, Keith shared many of my interests and was always ready to be a part of any adventure that was on offer. It was inevitable that Keith and I were destined to share those adventures.

My time aboard Markhor was up on the 16th of January 1979 when I left her in Sheerness.

I was due a considerable amount of leave from the previous year as well as time served on Markhor. However, I received telephone call in early March from fleet personnel asking if I would cut short my leave in order to relieve the third mate of the Port Chalmers when she arrived in Istanbul.

I enquired if any other reliefs would be flying out. Among the short list I was given was one name that stood out: Keith Jarrett.

My next trip to sea was going to be the start of the biggest adventure of them all.

CERTIFICATE OF COMPETENCY

AS

SECOND MATE No.1.2.1.2.31

OF A FOREIGN-GOING SHIP

To ——— Nicholas James Eliason ———

WHEREAS you have been found duly qualified to fulfil the duties of Second Mate of a Foreign-going Ship in the Merchant Navy, the Board of Trade in exercise of their powers under the Merchant Shipping Acts and of all other powers enabling them in that behalf hereby grant you this Certificate of Competency.

Dated this 9th day of October 1978

Countersigned

Registrar General.

An Assistant Secretary of the Board of Trade

REGISTERED AT THE OFFICE OF THE REGISTRAR GENERAL OF SHIPPING AND SEAMEN

Triumph

Aqaba, December 1978

Chapter 35

Behind The Iron Curtain

From seaward, the coast bordering the north-eastern Black Sea loomed ahead as Port Chalmers approached the Russian port of Novorossiysk.

From a distance, the coastline rose sharply to the foothills of the Caucasus mountain range. At the foot of the hills a strip of grey marked our destination.

We spent thirty-six hours at anchor waiting our turn to enter the port with this enigmatic view.

Immediately prior to joining Port Chalmers, I had obtained a Russian phrase book from W. H. Smith and had studied this mysterious language seriously since leaving home.

Fortunately the Russian Pilot who came aboard could speak good English. Although puzzled at my "zdrasvootya", he seemed impressed at the attempt and diplomatically avoided laughing.

On nearing the entrance to Novorossiysk harbour, the strip of grey became rows of multi-storey buildings. They would benefit from a lick of paint. Ahead of these were numerous cranes and moored vessels of all kinds.

Blimey! What a bleak-looking place. It was March 17th 1979.

The leaden sky matched the dark sea and doubtless added to the sombre outline of the buildings.

But this was Soviet Russia during the Leonid Brezhnev era. No Manhattan bright lights awaited. In fact, Clacton in mid winter would appear more attractive.

As Third Mate I was to remain on the bridge assisting Captain Webber and the Russian pilot until safely tied up alongside.

On approaching the quayside, I saw Russian soldiers who would remain on guard at the gangway and each end of the ship during our seventeen-day stay.

Carried in the ship's holds were sixteen thousand tons of frozen New Zealand mutton for delivery. In any port equipped to discharge such a cargo, we would expect to be away within a few days.

Did I mention that this was Soviet Russia? Instead of conveyor belts, the Russians would be using buckets on the end of poorly maintained cranes operated by some of the toughest-looking women I had ever seen.

From the bridge I went down to the gangway where I was to meet Valentina, the liaison official during our visit. She could also speak fluent English so the phrase book was again returned to my jacket pocket.

Valentina informed me that members of the ship's company were welcome at the seamen's club situated just outside the dock gates. However, we would need to exchange our identity cards for a shore pass if we left the ship and all other ventures were restricted.

Weeks virtually confined to our floating prison? To cap it all, I would be working twelve-hour shifts starting at midnight that same night until the discharge was completed. It was already six p.m. I would need to shower, be ready for that evening meal and try to get some sleep as there had been very little of that since joining the ship. Happy days.

By midnight I had the hatches open on the cargo holds and waited for work to begin. Russian workers eventually shuffled aboard and began the discharge. It was a long night. It was cold. It was just me and the Russians. It also happened to be my 25th birthday.

Thoughts of finishing at noon were shattered when problems were discovered with deck machinery. When rectified, it was evening time. A scrub and grub were required.

"We can go ashore Nick!" said Keith Jarratt, a shipmate from a previous trip aboard the Markhor. He was standing in my doorway as I was dressing for dinner. He had with a big grin on his face.

"Forget it, Keith. I'm starting at midnight again and am already shattered."

"But it's your birthday. We HAVE to celebrate!"

The seaman's club that Valentina spoke of was austere. There was a large empty room on the ground floor that could be a dance hall. Adjacent to that was a reading room. Empty.

On the first floor, however, was a dimly lit canteen. Also empty except for a figure at one end. Standing behind a bar!

Keith and I sat down at the table nearest this bar and out came the phrasebook.

"Dva peeva pazhousta" I said. (This just happened to be the very first phrase I had studied).

Amazingly it worked and two bottles of the local brew appeared.

"Would you like glasses with that?" said the bartender fluently.

We did and found the beer to be quite palatable. Shame there was no atmosphere.

However, within twenty minutes, the canteen door opened and two attractive young women entered. They sat on a table at the far end of the room. I looked at Keith. Keith looked at me.

My first thought was that if these were local residents then perhaps not all Russian women were brought up to be crane drivers or shot-putters.

Then Valentina, the liaison official entered and saw us. She came over to where Keith and I were sitting and asked if we wouldn't mind joining the two girls at the other table as they were students of English and hoped to practice the language.

Naturally we didn't want to seem rude, so agreed.

Valentina introduced us. "Ludmilla and Tonya, this is Keith and Nick".

And so began a relationship that was to last twenty years.

Chapter 36

Behind The Iron Curtain 2

Tonya and Ludmilla were students of English. Keith and I were now students of Tonya and Ludmilla.

Although smiling with enthusiasm, it quickly became apparent that both girls struggled with English and Tonya's dictionary only contributed to painfully slow dialogue.

This evening was going to be a challenge. The drinks were flowing but conversation was not.

Of course! The Penguin!

The phrase book was produced from my back pocket and suddenly I became fluent in Russian.

I couldn't find any jokes in the book but within minutes both girls were laughing hysterically.

Okay, so my pronunciation may require a little work but it was a start.

At this time, Russians were not noted for their sense of humour - which isn't surprising considering average living conditions - so phrases akin to:

"My home is full of dead sheep" or "Does my cell have a view?" caused more than a few smiles.

Gradually the room filled with crew members from Port Chalmers and a party atmosphere developed.

The evening flew by and ended too soon. I was needed back on board for the midnight shift and it was getting late.

Reluctantly, the four of us parted company but agreed to meet again the following evening at the seaman's club.

Although it got off to a dull start, my twenty-fifth birthday was one I shall not forget.

I couldn't make the club that following evening due to shift changes. When I met up with Tonya on the 20th, I discovered that she had practised English sentences that were unexpectedly flattering.

Whenever we could during the rest of our stay, the four of us would meet up. We were able on two occasions to take advantage of organised coach tours. One a general tour of Novorossiysk, when Tonya pointed out where she lived and the other to a wine-producing region.

Turns out, the area around Novorossiysk was the premier wine-producing region in the whole U.S.S.R. Before that tour, Keith and I had made do with locally brewed beer. After that tour nothing but the local Sovietskoye Champanskoye was good enough. It was cheaper too!

On 3rd April our stay in Russia came to an end.

It wasn't easy saying our goodbyes. Sometimes you just meet people with whom you wish you could maintain contact. But this was Russia and a goodbye was final. Tonya and I exchanged photographs. It was all rather emotional.

Port Chalmers was to sail for New Zealand which had always been a favourite Port Line destination. However, as the port of Novorossiysk slowly disappeared to our stern, I couldn't help feeling a twinge of sadness.

It was a pleasant enough voyage to New Zealand. Navigating through The Bosporous, Eastern Mediterranean, Suez and then across the Indian Ocean. Sharks, dolphins and the odd albatross were frequent companions. It was adventure that I had signed up for.

Now it was no secret among the officers and crew that a certain interest had developed between me and a young Russian girl whilst in our last port. Soon, they said, all will be forgotten when we hit the Kiwi coast. Preparation for the arrival parties were already underway!

On 3rd of May I was on my morning bridge watch. The coast of North Island, New Zealand had just come into view through the morning haze. The sun had been up for some time and a beautiful day was in the offing. By that evening we should be among the bright lights of Auckland.

The wheelhouse door behind me opened and Captain Webber came in clutching a piece of paper.

"Just got news from head office in London. I think you'll like this, Nick. We are to load mutton for the Russians". He smiled and continued:

"Most likely Novo-whatever-it-is. Again!"

Chapter 37

Kiwi Interlude

Port Line Limited was one of the more famous shipping companies within the British Merchant Navy. The vessels designed and built for Port Line were considered among the finest in the world.

Port Chalmers, along with her sister, Port Caroline, were the largest, finest and last to be built.

Nick Eliason had been the very last Port Line deck cadet.

Port Line and its rival company, Blue Star, had been in the frozen meat shipping industry for decades. New Zealand was a major supplier and regular destination for their ships.

The reputation that had been built over the years between New Zealanders and Port Line crews was legendary.

For a week prior to arrival, our crew had been preparing for a party. The crew bar, which was much larger than the officer's equivalent, was tucked away at the ship's stern immediately below the main deck and ran the full beam.

Whilst on the New Zealand coast, it had become a tradition for the ship's captain and officers to turn a blind eye to the bar antics of the crew - provided they were in a fit enough state to 'turn-to' when required.

"Me and the lads have had a chat. You and the 'second leckie' will be welcome to join us in our bar tonight" said the young bridge watchman to me as I was looking down at the quayside from the starboard bridge wing. He obviously felt it necessary to add: "We won't be inviting any of the other officers though!"

An honour indeed. The crew always seemed to have more fun in their bar than we did in ours.

As the gangway was being lowered to the quayside, I could not fail to notice the group of young women that had already congregated. The first of them stepped onto the gangway before it had even landed on solid ground. Wolf whistles and cheering could be heard from the afterdeck.

We had arrived alright!

That evening I stepped over the sill of the crew bar doorway with Keith not far behind.

Dire Straits had just released their 'Sultans Of Swing' album and it could be heard from the dock gates. There was an embarrassing cheer from within and a cold can of Leopard lager was handed to me. Before I could reach a bar stool, I had another can in the other hand. Looking round, I saw numerous young ladies among our lads whose obvious aim was to enjoy themselves.

The party had begun. This could be quite a night I thought. And it was!

Now at this point I feel it best to move on. The phrase 'What happens on the Kiwi coast remains on the Kiwi coast' seems most appropriate.

Suffice to say, the entire coastal was a stark contrast to weeks spent at sea or in less exciting destinations.

On May 13th I hired a car for a tour of Northland with Keith. We visited Wellsford, Helensville and Bays.

On May 15th we departed Auckland bound for Napier. We had female passengers aboard.

When not required to work, evenings in Napier were invariably spent at The Cabanna or Silver Spade nightclubs. More happy days. I wonder if those clubs still exist.

The partying ended on 26th May when Port Chalmers fired up her twin engines and edged away from our berth in Napier aided by tugs.

What memories we were to take away.

On the quayside, I saw some of the girls that had somehow remained with us for our entire stay.

All looked rather upset as they waved us goodbye. Maybe we would return. Maybe not.

Navigational charts had been prepared for our passage to Aden. From Aden we would complete the charts for our Russian destination. We waited. Head office had yet to confirm where that destination would be. Perhaps Novorossiysk?

Confirmation came before we reached Aden. Novorossiysk It was!

Port Chalmers bunkered in Aden before navigating The Red Sea, followed by northbound transit of The Suez Canal.

On June 22nd while at anchor off Istanbul, Captain Webber left the ship and was replaced by Captain Packwood.

As we got under way to transit The Bosporous en route to Novorossisyk, our new captain, along with the pilot and myself were in the wheelhouse.

Captain Packwood turned to me and lowered his binoculars.

"What's this unpronounceable port that we are heading for like, Nick? I understand it's bloody awful".

"It's bloody awful, sir" I replied - but I couldn't hide the grin!

Chapter 38

Return To Novorossiysk

The sun was shining as Port Chalmers made fast to number fourteen berth in Novorossisysk.

It was Saturday, 23rd of June 1979 and in the intervening period since we had been away, there had been a transformation in this part of the world - a world which was generally off limits to western visitors.

The climate had become Mediterranean resulting in a welcome atmosphere.

Russian soldiers still kept guard over us from the quayside and the buildings still hadn't been treated to a coat of paint but the grey concrete structures now appeared brighter in the sunlight.

After securing the stern mooring ropes and placing rat guards, I went to my cabin for a shower. En route, I bumped into Derek Lax, the First Mate who said to me with smile on his face "Just been told that the Russkies won't be starting 'till Monday - so it looks like we've got the rest of the weekend off. See you in the bar!"

A weekend off! Unheard of!

The shower was completed in record time and I did make it to the bar for a swift, but my mind was focused on the seaman's club just outside the dock gates.

At the foot of the gangway, I exchanged my seaman's card for a shore pass with the soldiers stationed there. I guess this enabled the Soviet authorities to monitor our movements to their satisfaction. We had been warned that any infringement of this privilege would result in its withdrawal and the individual would not be allowed further shore leave.

Yep, this was a different world.

I passed through the heavily guarded dock gates and made for the club. Would Tonya still want to meet? How was I to make contact? I didn't have a telephone number or an address. Not to mention the communication hurdle. Perhaps someone at the club could help?

I needn't have worried. On arrival at the club and sitting at the same table where we had first met was Tonya. What a feeling! No words were necessary.

At this time, Tonya worked in the engineering department of the Novorossiysk shipping offices.

As such, she had access to shipping movements and probably knew before me of our arrival.

Tonya's English had improved far beyond my Russian and with 'Sovietskoye Champanskoye' flowing freely, communication hardly seemed a problem anymore.

The facilities of the club were also exploited by other members of our crew who had drifted in during the evening. Some also experienced the debilitating effect of the local 'vino' that incidentally, could only be purchased by the bottle. It appeared that nearly everyone had a glass in one hand and a bottle in the other.

By late evening it became clear that the staff wanted to close the premises and so the club's customers reluctantly started to leave. Many were singing.

Tonya and I said our goodbye at the door of a taxi and agreed to meet again the following day.

She handed me a piece of paper which had an address written in green ink. I still have that piece of paper.

My return to the ship did not go smoothly.

A queue had formed at the gangway while our dock passes were being exchanged for our seaman's cards. The process was unduly slow as the more inebriated crew members fumbled for documents and Russian soldiers checked each individual against his card photograph.

For a reason that remains unknown, one of our crew must have taken it upon himself to survey the ship's side from the waterline. We heard an almighty splash and investigation revealed he had fallen into the dock between the quayside and the ship. A very dangerous situation.

At this point the queue broke as crew members raced up the gangway to throw ropes, lifebuoys and anything else that could float into the dock for the hapless soul to grab hold of. Even the painting barge that was attached to our afterdeck crane was swung out over the ship's side.

The mayhem caused a panic among the Russian soldiers and soon there were dozens that materialised waving AK assault rifles. Perhaps they believed that some of the locals were among our crew and attempting to seek political asylum?

"Don't shoot! There' a man overboard!" - was not a phrase I could find in my book.

Fortunately, the Russian officer who appeared, assessed the situation and succeeded in calming his charges. The soldiers now just watched as we hauled the crewman to safety.

Jock, the Scottish fourth engineer, may have been a very lucky man that evening but he had a bit of a drink problem. At least this was the explanation that eventually satisfied the Russian authorities as to the reason for his late night swim. Even so, it took hours to sort the identity documents and convince the Russians that we hadn't assisted potential stowaways.

That night I 'turned in' with an overpowering feeling of apprehension. Would the Russian authorities now withdraw our shore leave privileges?

Chapter 39

Summer Special

Sunday 24th June 1979 dawned bright and sunny. Sleep had been at a premium but I was still able to make the saloon for breakfast. I needed to know if shore leave was still permitted.

No one I spoke to had any information. Jock was on the mend which was welcome news and nothing else seemed to matter at that time. Well, to me at least, there were other matters.

Around mid morning Valentina, the Russian liaison official, came aboard to speak with the captain.

I think I must have been the second person aboard to learn of developments.

Apparently, Jock's attempt at seeking attention had an unexpected effect on our Russian hosts. Not only was further shore leave permitted, but Valentina had arranged coach tours for anyone that may be interested in seeing more than the interior of the seaman's club.

Maybe I was pushing my luck, but that afternoon I handed my piece of paper that had Tonya's address written on it to the driver of a taxi who I found conveniently parked some way from the dock gates. He looked at me as if I was mad. I showed him a ten-rouble note. The driver shrugged and indicated to me to get in.

After fifteen minutes, the taxi stopped outside a concrete apartment block. The driver pointed in the direction of a doorway and pocketed my ten roubles. I got out of the taxi and tried to explain, with the aid of my phrase book, that I would like him to wait while I checked out the address. He looked at me again as if I was mad and sped off with at least a full day's earnings in his pocket.

At this point I felt rather alone.

"Gde kvatirye vossyem-chetirye pazhauoosta?" The woman in the hallway looked at me as if I was mad. I was beginning to think I was. I showed her my piece of paper and her face lit up.

She pointed to the stairwell. Within minutes, I was standing outside a rather solid-looking door numbered 94. I knocked. When the door opened, Tonya stood with an expression of disbelief.

I was ushered inside and could tell she was pleased, yet puzzled, to see me. I met Tonya's mother, Zena for the first time. Tonya's father, Yuli, was not at home.

The whole afternoon and evening was spent together, walking through the town and by the sea. I was developing a liking for this port, and in particular, one of it's residents. I think that resident shared similar feelings.

By nature, I discovered, Russians walk a lot. By the evening's end, we were back at the dock gates and parting company once again. I saw Tonya into a taxi and noticed the driver had a familiar face.

Work on board began in earnest the following day. I was lucky enough to negotiate the eight am to eight pm shift with Ian Avis, the second mate. This meant that I was free to rendezvous with Tonya each evening. We became regulars at the Hunter's Lodge and Brigantina restaurants in town. My spoken Russian was improving resulting in fewer suspicious looks from locals.

Feelings deepened. On Thursday, 28th of June 1979, I discussed with Tonya the possibilities of marriage between a Russian citizen and a foreigner. Although unexpected, she didn't seem too surprised. She stated that it would be extremely difficult. She knew of only one previous successful case. So almost unheard of - but possible.

I suggested she made no hasty decisions but to give the possibility some thought. I would discuss this outrageous proposal with her another time.

How long should I wait to make a proposal? A week? Five days? Three days? No, it would have to be twenty-four hours. Less - if we met again sooner.

On the Friday evening Tonya and I met as arranged outside the Neptune cinema. I was early but she was already waiting. I wasn't interested in the film. It was in Russian. Instead, we took a long walk along the sea front which was now becoming quite familiar to me.

Little was said at first. Eventually I asked Tonya if she had considered the previous evening's discussion. She said she had. I asked her if she thought it may be possible for us to get married. She said she thought it might be. I asked her if it were possible, would she like to marry me?

In a very Russian sort of way, she replied "yes".

Although I couldn't appreciate the full implications of that modest conversation, I was inwardly ecstatic.

Now began the biggest challenge of my life……

Chapter 40

Last Of The Summer Wine.

Maybe it was the heat. The discharge of our cargo was mind-numbingly slow. The crew of the Port Chalmers had had enough of Russia and wanted to move on. Perfectly understandable.

On the other hand - I was delighted. The discharge was to drag on for another two weeks!

On 30th of June 1979, Tonya and other Russian girls from the Seaman's Club attended a special dinner aboard. This had the approval of the Novorossiysk authorities and confirmed that relations between the two nations could be more than cordial.

Although having to work long hours, I was able to take advantage of every minute of spare time.

On 1st of July there was a coach trip and picnic at a local lake. Being Russia, there wasn't a lot of pic to nic, so our Chief Steward produced an enormous hamper containing delicacies I was unaware we had aboard. We went swimming. I still have the photographs.

Perhaps we were becoming too familiar with Russian hospitality or perhaps blame could be attributed to the powerful 'Sovietskoye Champanskoye' but in either case, there was a minor infringement of privilege on one occasion when returning to the ship after an evening spent at the Seaman's Club.

Having passed through the security building at the dock gate, which involved a close scrutiny by security personnel, a small group of crew including myself witnessed a diesel goods train lumbering towards an open gate across the railway line. The lumbering was just a little faster than walking speed and the train displayed inviting steps on each of the wagons.

For no other reason than it seemed like fun at the time, I jumped up onto the nearest wagon and held on. Two of my companions must have had similar thoughts as they followed suit. The train passed through the gate and picked up speed. Blimey! What now? The longer I hesitated, the faster the train. We had covered several hundred metres when I saw a patch of reasonably soft-looking ground up ahead. I waited, then jumped. Big ouch! Not like Hollywood at all. Fortunately nothing seemed broken. Then - bigger ouch! One of my companions landed on top of me. We rolled around but eventually managed to stand. We were covered in filth. There was no sign of companion number three.

On the limp back to the security building at the gate, I brushed the filth off as best I could and presented myself to the guard as If it was his fault he was seeing double.

Nothing was said at the time but it transpired that our third companion was held for a short interrogation when he returned more than an hour later.

On 8th of July I was invited to Tonya's apartment on Nabarezhnaya Street where I met her brother, Roman, for the first time. Nice lad.

On the 10th - another picnic. Russians like to picnic. We went to an area known as Little Land. This was hallowed ground for Russians as it was the site of a major struggle against the Germans in World War Two. As a result of the bitter fighting that took place, Nonorossiysk became nominated by Stalin as a 'Hero City'.

Keith and Ludmilla came too and soon we found some comfortable old shell holes. These remain as memorials. I learned quite a lot that evening while in a shell hole.

However, time was running out. Discharge was due to finish early on the 15th and so the previous evening was to be my last run ashore. How was I to say goodbye again? I knew that Tonya felt the same. Although I had promised to return in the vain hope of somehow getting married, both of us knew the odds were stacked against such an outrageous plan.

So it was with a heavy heart that I left Tonya at the dock gate. Perhaps that final wave would be the last time we would see each other....

Port Chalmers slipped her moorings at six am on that following morning. The crew were happy, they had been told that we are bound for Falmouth - and home.

As I watched the Russian coast slowly ebb into the distance, I could only think of returning as soon as possible. Was a return even possible? I had no way of knowing.

But I was determined to find out.

Chapter 41

Uncharted Waters

A t 7 am on the 24th July 1979, Port Chalmers arrived at Falmouth.

The world's largest refrigerated cargo ship had no cargo to discharge and, due to changes in the shipping industry at that time, was laid-up in the River Fal to await further instructions.

Containerisation was seen as the future, and from now on, proud ships such as the Chalmers would be relegated to tramps. All rather sad.

I was to go home on leave along with most of the crew. Before leaving, I was handed a letter written by my dad on 17th of the month replying to my intention to marry. I have kept that letter.

The train journey from Falmouth to Knebworth seemed unending. My mind was wholly occupied with the immediate future and how to plan a return visit to Russia.

By 11 pm I was home. After the hugs, I sat down with my mum and dad who subjected me to a barrage of questions akin to The Spanish Inquisition. As to the immediate future, I had no answers.

The answers began to materialise two days later when I made the first of many pilgrimages to the Soviet Consulate at 5 Kensington

Palace Gardens in London. This was an imposing building, surrounded by tall iron railings and festooned with security cameras.

Frequently in the weeks to follow, the staff at the consulate would find me sitting on their steps, reading the latest copy of 'Bike' magazine, awaiting my turn to be invited in for discussion.

Just as frequently, I was told "Soviet citizens are not permitted to marry foreign nationals unless there are exceptional circumstances".

Well, I thought, let's make this an exceptional circumstance!

To be fair to the Russians, they did listen to my plight and supplied me with heaps of reading material - some of which was in English - but it was made clear that further discussion on the matter would have to be initiated by higher authority.

So I went to a higher authority.

On 23rd of August, I managed to get an audience with a Mr Whitcombe of The Foreign Office.

After lengthy discussion, Mr Whitcombe seemed hooked. What fun! An opportunity to extricate a Soviet national! Far more exciting than the everyday office routine.

As a result of this visit, a small team of rather imaginative but competent civil servants were formed to handle my case.

Now at last, there was hope. Without detailing all the paperwork, telephone calls and visits that were to follow - some of which took place on a diplomatic level between the Foreign Office and Soviet Consulate - a plan was developing.

On 5th September, travel arrangements were agreed for my return to Russia.

On 28th September, I collected a visa from Intourist, the Russian travel agency, which would permit me entry to Moscow as a tourist. I also forwarded the required marriage documents to the Foreign Office for transmission to the British Consul in Moscow. Soon I would be on my way!

Although not as soon as I had hoped, for there were still numerous bureaucratic hurdles to jump.

On 30th September, my paid leave expired. I was able to negotiate an unpaid absence from Cunard, since it transpired that the Fleet Personnel department were avid followers of my progress. I was promised my job would remain available until I returned...... If I returned!

However, it was a sobering thought to realise I was now unemployed and without income until I was able to renew my contract.

Time dragged on until all the organisations involved in my mission were satisfied that the necessary documentation was complete.

Needless to say, regular correspondence between Tonya and myself had ensured that my arrival in Russia was imminent. I have kept all Tonya's letters. (Most have really interesting stamps).

On 14th November, I received a telegram from Tonya. During the the months of waiting, she had also endeavoured to obtain the documentation she believed necessary to proceed with wedding arrangements. The future still remained agonisingly uncertain but she had done all she could considering the lack of precedent. She had arrived in Moscow.

Now it was my turn.

Chapter 42

Mission To Moscow

An early start on Monday, the 19th November 1979 found me standing on Knebworth railway station platform waiting for the six minutes past six train to King's Cross. The cold and damp of the morning added to the apprehension of the journey that lay ahead.

Flight BA 708 from Heathrow to Moscow was on schedule although almost empty. Other passengers all appeared to be business people. There were no obvious tourists onboard and I concluded that I may be the only one.

I enjoy flying but on this occasion it was literally a flight into the unknown.

The cabin bag I had with me contained a heavy file of documents that had been largely compiled by the Foreign Office in London. If I had forgotten anything then it would have to stay forgotten.

Flying due east meant that It was dark by the time we landed at Sheremetyeva Airport in Moscow.

Probably due to the lack of travellers, the formalities at the airport didn't take as long as I had expected - although I was subject to a game of stare by a uniformed immigration official.

The arrivals hall was also nearly empty. Where was everybody? Where was Intourist? Was my Russian good enough to summon a taxi?

Then I caught sight of a slim figure that was unmistakably Tonya's.

The meeting was understandably emotionally charged. Tonya's usually pale complexion began to colour and the rapidity of questions fired at me indicated that she was rather pleased that I had honoured my promise to return. The feeling of excitement was mutual.

A dozen empty taxis were available outside the airport to take us to my Intourist Hotel. Just as well - the temperature in Moscow was well below freezing. There was snow on the ground and a light snow was falling.

Part one of 'Operation Mad Dog' was complete.

Soviet Authorities would not allow Tonya to accompany me inside the hotel, so instead, we found a small cafe/bar close by to catch up on four month's worth of absence. More importantly, we could discuss our next step. It was late when we parted company but this time we knew we could meet the following day. Tonya was to stay with some relatives living in this vast city.

Next morning the view of Moscow from my hotel window on Gorky Street was completely obscured by thick ice covering the entire window. Better dig out my warm socks.

At ten o'clock I met with Tonya outside the hotel. Blimey! It was bitterly cold. I was beginning to realise why most Russians wore thick fur coats and hats. I really needed to get hold of one of those ubiquitous ushankas that all the soldiers were issued. There were soldiers everywhere. However, our mission that day was to visit the British Consul to exchange certain documents and discuss progress, so any thoughts of shopping would have to wait.

In a very English way, tea and biscuits were provided at the consulate while the aforesaid discussion was taking place. All seemed very convivial until it was made clear that if a marriage was to take place, then according to Soviet law, the wedding must take place in the district of residence of one of the parties concerned. Tonya and I looked at each other.

When we left the consulate we were in possession of all the necessary documents that I had supplied to the Foreign Office in London weeks previously. These had been forwarded to Moscow in time to be translated into Russian by consular staff. I was beginning to believe there could be light at the end of a long tunnel. Dare we allow ourselves some time to celebrate a little? For the rest of the day, after a visit to the Intourist office, we did just that.

So, it would appear, there would not be a wedding in Moscow as I had rather naively expected. Never mind, I'll just have to find a way to get to Novorossiysk - Tonya's home town. In the event, Intourist were only too happy to arrange a flight, hotel and visa to Sochi on the Black Sea coast. It was the nearest tourist-friendly town to Novorossiysk. The flight was scheduled for Thursday.

When I saw Tonya the next day, she looked drained of enthusiasm. The reason, she explained, was due to an error she had discovered on one of the documents. Unless corrected, the Soviet authorities would not permit marriage. What now? These papers had taken weeks of meticulous preparation. Would we fall at the last hurdle?

That day, Wednesday 21st of November, was a whirlwind. A replacement Certificate of No Impediment for Tonya had to be obtained. Somehow.

Then began a feverish rush back to the consulate. After explaining our dilemma, consular officials began a dialogue with The Soviet Ministry For Foreign Affairs. Soviet officials insisted on speaking to the Consul himself. However, the Consul was out until later in the day. The tunnel was lengthening and the light began to dim.

After an agonising wait for the Consul to return and take up the dialogue, I was finally given a letter, written in Russian and signed by the Consul.

"Take this to the Russians as quickly as you can. They are expecting you. Oh, and good luck!"

It was nearly four o'clock. The Ministry would close at five. The streets of Moscow were covered in snow and the evening rush had begun. The Metro was the quickest form of transport and we forced ourselves into a packed carriage.

With barely ten minutes to spare, we arrived at the gates but were turned away by armed guards.

There was a telephone number on the letter so we searched for a phone box. The only box in sight had a queue outside but something Tonya said made the line stand aside. The occupant was virtually pulled from the box. Now we couldn't find the right change. Back out of the box and ask for change. A ten kopek coin cost me five roubles but the call was finally made.

Back to the gates and the guards allowed us to pass after a serious verbal exchange that I didn't understand.

A young woman, waiting inside the Ministry, took the letter and hurried up a flight of stairs.

We waited. Employees began flooding past us after their day's work. Interior lights were being switched off. Then silence.

To our unimaginable relief, the young woman returned, she thrust a document into my hand and without saying a word, turned and hurried back up the stairs. Tonya and I stared at the document. Tonya's face lit up. At last we had everything we needed, all present and correct.

I was over the moon. Tonya was over the moon. The journey back to my hotel that night in the bitter cold went unnoticed.

The next morning I telephoned the Consul to thank him for his assistance and inform him of my intention to travel to Novorossiysk.

"Novorossiysk? On the Black Sea? Not possible, I'm afraid. You see - it is a naval base and as such, entry is not permitted to foreign tourists such as yourself. I should also give you fair warning that if you attempt to go to Novorossiysk, you make yourself liable to arrest by the Russians. In that event, I really don't think we will be able to intervene".

Another bombshell had just dropped.

Chapter 43

Killing Time

'Operation Mad Dog' was dead. With defeat came a feeling of resignation bordering depression.

It was now Thursday, the 22nd of November 1979. Tonya had returned to Novorossiysk the previous evening and I was alone in Moscow. I had a flight booked to Sochi, a hotel reservation and a visa, so I made the decision to fly south. At least Tonya should be able to meet me in Sochi where we could make the most of the time we had left.

At 1.40 pm I boarded an Aeroflot Tupolev 154 for the journey and was rather surprised to find cages of livestock among the passengers. Not many Brits on this aeroplane I thought, looking around. The Tupolev sounded much louder than any other aircraft I had flown in and on the approach to Sochi, the pilot made a dramatic left turn and dived. We were now in an incredibly steep descent and some caged birds shot past my seat on their way towards the crew cabin.

The engines were screaming and I checked that both wings were still attached. Amazingly, none of the passengers seemed concerned so I assumed all was normal.

Some time later, I learned that Aeroflot pilots have previous military aircraft training, so our captain may well have been on a nostalgia trip.

At 6 pm I arrived at Hotel Kamelia. The sky was grey and threatening. The adjacent Black Sea was living up to its name. I was given keys, but on my way to the room, I saw no one.

After depositing my luggage, I went to the hotel's restaurant area which was deserted except for one couple dining at a corner table. They were Donn and Linda Mainer from Vancouver. I would get to know them quite well over the next few days. That evening I went for a long walk and was fortunate to find a post office that enabled a telegram to be sent to Tonya.

Friday was spent getting to know the town and the few other hotel occupants. However, it didn't seem like much of a holiday. I sent another telegram to Tonya and anxiously waited a reply.

Nothing materialised. Shashlik for dinner and a long conversation with Donn and Linda.

Saturday opened darkly overcast with continuous rain. The weather was mirroring my mood. I spent most of that day in my hotel room trying to absorb a copy of 'The Russians' by Hedrick Smith. Bad idea - nothing cheerful there. My anxiety was growing. Why had I not yet heard from Tonya? I was beginning to accept the inevitable. Marriage was now out of the question and even further contact with Tonya was diminishing. All that planning, preparation and effort had come to nothing. At least we had given it our best shot, although the thought was little consolation.

Then - a telegram! It was from Tonya and comprised three words: 'Will arrive Sunday'.

Perhaps coincidental with the telegram, Sunday opened fine and mild with sunshine at last.

After breakfast of semolina with salt, hard boiled egg and warm tea, I took another long walk along Sochi's beach and into town. I was killing time.

In the afternoon I took my book to the lounge/bar area and tried to read but my mind was else where. The lounge was empty as usual but occasionally the hotel manager would make an appearance. This was a pleasant woman in her mid forties with whom I had brief conversations since my arrival. Although I cannot remember her name, her English was quite good and she had shown an interest in my reason for being in Sochi. As it was obviously out of season, her hotel was almost empty of the tourists who would normally visit this internationally renowned health resort. So why would a single Englishman bother to visit?

So I told her the entire sorry story over a bottle of wine. I was mastering the art of killing time.

At 6pm that evening Tonya arrived in Sochi - but again, because of Soviet restrictions, she had to book into a different hotel. Nevertheless, we met in the town and spent the evening together.

The evening was fraught by strong and confusing emotion. The anxiety was clear from Tonya's expressions. In fact, she had been quite ill since our parting in Moscow and this was the reason why there was a communication delay. I explained that I was willing to try to return again next year. If Tonya could move to Moscow in the meantime, then we should have more success.

At least I now knew the procedure to follow and even had contacts at The Foreign Office.

Difficult as it was, none of my attempts to console Tonya were sufficient. She smiled, but I could tell she thought my offer was a forlorn hope. While in Novorossiysk, she had even been to the marriage registry. She had been told that the documentation was complete and they could help if we attended during the week.

However, without a visa being issued by the authorities it would be an insane risk for me to attempt to go there. Tonya was well aware of that. Arrest, or worse, imprisonment in the Soviet Union was not to be relished.

So it was that we parted again that evening and went to our respective hotels. Before going to my room, I called in at the bar. Sleep would be a tough call anyway. As well as a barman, the manageress was sitting nursing a drink. I was invited to sit with her. After a rather simple discussion in broken English about the evening's events, she leaned over to me and in a low voice, said "I have given your problem much thought. I can help. My brother is senior officer in KGB here in Sochi. I talk to him today. He get you twenty four hours visa for Novorossiysk on this 28th day. So now you go. Yes?"

I looked at her in disbelief. Could this be true? She seemed sincere.

"Shall we have another drink?" I said.

Chapter 44

A Brush With The KGB

The stairwell that led to the empty foyer of Hotel Kamelia was dimly lit. I had been awake all night waiting for a rendezvous with the notorious KGB. At ten minutes to five on the morning of the 28th of November 1979, I looked out of the foyer window onto the hotel driveway. In the darkness outside, barely illuminated by a single lamp, I could see heavy rain bouncing off the ground.

Ten minutes later, the headlights of a vehicle swept across the foyer windows and came to an abrupt halt. A shadowy figure stepped out from the passenger door and entered the hotel.

A heavily built man, rather scruffily dressed in a worn leather jacket, ushanka and military style trousers, fixed me with a stare.

"Eta Neek, Da?" He said.

"Da" I replied in fluent Russian.

He followed with "Die menya roublee Pazhaloosta."

I handed him an envelope containing two hundred roubles which he counted in front of me. He then reached into an inside pocket and produced an identity card. I recognised the cyrillic letters

KGB. Then he gave me the document that regenerated 'Operation Mad Dog'. It was a twenty-four hour visa to enter Novorossiysk!

The hotel manageress had been true to her word. She and her brother had arranged the rendezvous and had reversed the impossible. If she had been in that foyer she would have been subject to an enormous hug. Even so, I still couldn't help feeling a strong sense of anxiety.

The KGB man pointed to the car outside and beckoned me to go with him: "Pashlee, Neek. Na Novorossiysk. Eta ocheen dyelako!

I followed him and climbed into the back seat of a dark coloured Volga saloon. A second man, the driver, accelerated away from the hotel before I had even closed the door.

Next stop was to be the Leningrad Hotel in Sochi. Tonya was waiting at the appointed time to be collected. The Volga then sped off again, out of town and onto the coast road, heading north.

The three hundred kilometre journey took six hours. The coast road followed the contours of the Caucasus foothills which created numerous inclines and sharp turns. The road surface was poor with pot holes and loose gravel, causing the Volga to jolt and slide. The standard of driving also contributed to uncomfortable conditions for the passengers. Tonya became increasingly car sick.

At around midday, we arrived in the outskirts of Novorossiysk. The town looked as drab as it had done when I first saw it nine months previously. Except now I felt exhilaration at having made the pilgrimage without being a part of a ship's crew. It almost felt like coming home.

The Volga swiftly drove along the outlying streets in the direction of the port. Eventually we stopped outside a squat, grey building with a notice board outside proclaiming 'Atdyel Zags'.

This could be translated as 'Wedding Palace'. We had arrived!

I couldn't help thinking that this building didn't look much like a palace and on closer inspection a further notice stated that it was closed.

Tonya and I stepped out of the car and moved towards the building. Tonya could hardly stand due to the debilitating effects of the journey. And now, after all we had been through, our destiny may be thwarted since the only building in all of Russia that could enable our marriage was CLOSED!

Our KGB chaperone began laughing. He had reached the door of the palace before us. When Tonya saw this she ran, even in her condition, to the door. A second notice in smaller script, informed the reader that staff had left for lunch and would return at two pm.

It was now twelve-thirty, Yet more time to kill. Enough time to see the sights? A stroll around the local area would have to suffice. Not much to see here, besides, it was cold, dull and heavily overcast. Telephone calls were made and within thirty minutes Tonya's brother Roman and Luda, Tonya's best friend, met with us as we arrived back at the palace.

Our small group waited nervously outside the building with Tonya and Luda chatting incessantly. The driver of the Volga had vanished along with the car. I tried conversing with Roman and was met with smiles and furious nodding.

It was now almost two o'clock and we were not alone. Quite a large group of young men in Russian naval uniform and their girlfriends had gathered. They looked at me inquisitively. I was wearing full blue British merchant naval uniform and became an object of interest as an unusual sighting.

At two o'clock precisely, the doors of the palace were opened and the internal hallway was flooded by couples eager to get married.

The hall was lined with seats and we were all asked to sit and wait. A female staff member moved from couple to couple collecting completed application forms - Tonya had ours.

It occurred to me that photographs may be possible as I had kept hold of my Olympus camera. I showed the camera to Roman and our KGB man in the hope they could take some pictures if the impossible now became possible. Both were interested in being our official photographers but in the event, the KGB won. So a crash course in the use of a 35mm Olympus OM-1 followed.

There followed an anxious wait. Even at this late hour, we didn't know if we would be able to marry. Everything now hinged on the authorities being satisfied that all prescribed applications had been correctly completed with supporting documentation submitted.

After fifteen minutes, an office door at the end of the hallway opened and two middle-aged women, both wearing official sashes denoting their authority, approached Tonya and me. They asked us to confirm our names and then indicated that we follow them. So follow them we did.

We entered a large room with a grand table at one end. Above this was a large wall plaque displaying the hammer and sickle motif of the U.S.S.R. A brass strip had been set into the parquet floor which we were instructed to stand behind. Classical Russian music was heard from a gramophone player at the rear of the room. Roman and Luda accompanied us as witnesses and the KGB man stood inside the door.

'Operation Mad Dog' was back on!

Chapter 45

Mission Accomplished

With sombre classical music filling the palace hall, the official appointed to preside over our wedding looked at me with a matching stare. What was she thinking? Why wasn't she smiling?

Was something wrong? Without saying a word, she turned her attention to Tonya and treated her to a similar look. There was silence.

The official then stepped forward and began a dialogue which I couldn't understand. She sounded extremely formal but at the end of her speech she gave me that same stare. I think she may have asked me a question judging by the inflexion in her voice.

I simply said "Da".

For all I knew I could have just admitted to being a foreign spy. However, my answer seemed to do the trick as she then turned her attention to Tonya.

Tonya was able to reply in more detail which created what I thought may be the beginning of a smile on the official's face. The feeling of relief was tempered when the official began speaking to me again. Each time she paused I replied "Da". Nothing could stop me now - I felt as if I was deeply involved in the conversation.

Then unexpectedly, the wedding procedure stalled. The official stood in front of me holding a salver. There was an uncomfortable silence which was only broken when Tonya said: "Ring!"

Of course! In my uniform pocket was the wedding ring which I had matched at a jeweller in England from a piece of twisted copper wire fashioned to the size of Tonya's ring finger. Tonya had posted it to me while I was on leave.

I placed the ring on the salver but was unaware that custom dictated I should have placed two rings so that they could be ceremoniously exchanged at this point. I never even thought of having a wedding ring myself. The official looked as confused as I was but made due allowance and after another disapproving glare, I was allowed to place the ring on Tonya's finger.

Was that it? Were we now married? The answer came in the form of music. The gramophone record had been changed to a much lighter, happier piece of classical Russian and even the official was now smiling. This was followed by encouragement from our official to perform the regulation Russian wedding kiss.

Next came an invitation to sign an enormous wedding register. I was so relieved at the realisation that so much effort had finally resulted in success that I almost snatched the pen from the official's hand. As I bent to write, I was stopped. The other registrar pulled me upright. Tonya explained to me that another custom requires a standing posture when signing formal documents.

I was on a rather steep learning curve.

Tonya then signed and our signatures were witnessed by Roman and Luda.

Throughout, the man from the KGB had been taking shots with my camera but at no time did the flash unit activate despite my frantic sign language to switch it on. I could only hope there may be an image or two that would serve as a record of events.

Back into the hallway outside and another couple were ushered past us to repeat the procedure.

Tonya and Luda engaged in an excited babble while I tried to explain the workings of my camera once again to the KGB. A short while later, a member of staff came to me and handed me a grey, passport-sized document. I opened it and saw that it had been completed in beautiful hand-written cyrillic script. This was our certificate of marriage. Mission finally accomplished - Operation Mad Dog was a success! What relief! We even had the support of the Russian Navy as I found myself shaking hands with complete strangers in the hallway. Photographs were needed.

The rest of the afternoon was spent with Tonya's family at their apartment on Nabarezhnaya Street. The driver of the Volga had materialised and was accompanied by several bottles of vodka. Tonya's mother, Zena, had prepared an enormous buffet and, in company with Roman and Luda, we all sat around a dining table. The atmosphere could not be more convivial.

Both KGB men and Tonya's father Yuri, seemed to engage in a drinking challenge - which was a major concern as we still had to return to Sochi with one of the challengers driving the Volga. Maybe it was just as well time was short since it allowed Tonya to convince the KGB that we needed to make a move while they could still stand. The driver was nominated the challenge winner and he seemed happy with that.

The journey back to Sochi was even worse than in the morning. It was now dark and the driver failed to notice many of the holes in the road. His vision would have been impaired by the poor headlighting and no doubt the quantity of vodka he had made friends with. Our lives were in his hands which was not a pleasant feeling. I was just hoping he saw the dangerous bends in time.

Tonya was again car sick and it came as an enormous relief when we finally reached Sochi and Hotel Kamelia.

In fairness to our KGB friends, we could never have managed without them. From now on, my concept of this enigmatic and immensely powerful Russian organisation would change.

Both Tonya and I were utterly exhausted when we waved goodbye to to the rapidly disappearing Volga, but nonetheless elated at what had been achieved that day. We had even made it back to Sochi with thirty minutes to spare on my visa so what could top that?

To top that was the welcome acceptance by the hotel manageress that we could now both stay together in her hotel!

Marriage Certificate

Chapter 46

Moscow Moon

My Sochi visa was due to expire on 30th November which allowed a whole day to be spent in and around Hotel Kamelia. Although the hotel was almost empty of guests, the day was one of champagne and celebration with our friends among the staff and the Mainers from Vancouver.

Tonya was recovering from the previous day's ordeal and I was feeling the benefit of an enormous weight having been lifted. The copious quantities of champagne also contributed to a strong sense of well-being.

Yes, the future was certainly looking far brighter than it did just forty-eight hours previously. A telegram was sent home to update my family.

During pre-dinner drinks, Donn Mainer asked the inevitable question relating to the Soviet authorities stance on granting Tonya permission to leave Russia. A moot point and I think he realised immediately that further dialogue on the subject could spoil the evening.

The fact remained that a marriage certificate was no guarantee that a Soviet citizen would be granted an exit visa to live abroad. I knew this from my discussions with the Foreign Office.

However, the certificate did provide grounds for an application. Again, our future together depended on decisions being made by government officials in Russia over whom we had no control.

The afternoon flight from Sochi to Moscow was delayed due to bad weather. Once airborne, Tonya began to feel airsick and sat quietly for most of the four-hour journey. We landed in darkness and found Moscow to be covered in a thick blanket of snow. At half past eight our taxi pulled up outside the Leningradski Hotel which had been pre-booked by Intourist.

It is worth mentioning that Intourist at this time was the sole, state controlled agency dealing with foreign travellers to Russia. As such, they were able to monitor movements and provide accommodation that was off limits to Soviet citizens.

Hotel Leningradski was therefore off limits to Tonya and there followed an interesting debate at the hotel reception. Even the production of the marriage certificate did little to placate the staff who were adamant that Tonya must find alternative accommodation. It would be an understatement to say I became a little irritated. This caused staff to seek advice from a superior authority with the eventual result that we were given a small, single room high up in the building.

I considered this to be a victory for common sense. In retrospect however, the hotel staff had probably never been faced with such a unique situation.

The following morning, the 1st of December, was to be my last full day in Russia as my visa was due to expire on the 2nd. Fortunately, and not surprisingly, Intourist had an office in the huge foyer of the hotel through which I was able to extend my visa until the 6th of December. Intourist were only too happy to do this as foreign visitors were at a premium and a charge of thirty pounds per extra day would be a welcome addition to their coffers.

So now a six day honeymoon had become a reality! What plans to make? We were now both tourists in Russia's great capital.

Tonya wanted to go shopping, so that afternoon was spent travelling to various stores on the Moscow Metro. Shopping is not a favourite pastime of mine but I was greatly impressed by the underground transport system. It was not only spotlessly clean but constructed with vast amounts of marble and lit by enormous chandeliers. This was one of Stalin's architectural masterpieces and would put the London Underground to shame.

December 2nd was spent sightseeing. Even though it was bitterly cold and snow covered almost everything, I was fascinated by the city and its culture. On returning to Hotel Leningradski, we were hugely surprised to find that Intourist had seen fit to move us from our original room to an enormous double bedroom - as good as any Hollywood bridal suite. Being au-fait with all the Bond films, I cautiously checked behind wall ornaments and table lamps looking for bugs - but, rather disappointingly, found none.

In order to progress an application for Tonya to leave Russia, it was necessary to register our marriage with the British Consul and request correspondence to begin between the British and Soviet authorities. Therefore a large part of the following day was spent at the consulate. Consular staff agreed to draft a letter of invitation for Tonya to come to England but it was made clear, once again, that it would be up to the Soviet authorities to consider an exit visa for her. No one seemed able to state when, or even if, that may be.

"I don't suppose you would consider settling in Russia, Mr Eliason?" I was asked at one point.

I didn't answer - I think my glare was sufficient.

December 4th was very pleasant. At nine o'clock we were in Red Square and able to tour The Kremlin and its armoury. Very impressive. I could have spent all day there. I was able to acquire an ushanka fur hat which contributed to making the weather outside more tolerable. Touring can be tiring, so much of the afternoon was spent lazing at our hotel. Later that day, theatre tickets were booked via Intourist for a performance the following evening.

My last full day in Moscow included another visit to the British Consulate where I was able to collect a copy of the agreed letter of invitation. This had been typed in Russian but Tonya was pleased with its content so we thanked the consular staff for all their help. In return we were wished luck.

Luck had been with us so far. Would it remain with us until Tonya was allowed to leave Russia?

That evening was spent at the Kremlin theatre. The world-famous Bolshoi Theatre Company were to perform The Rimsky Korsakov opera 'The Czar's Fiancee'. Very good it was but I couldn't understand a word of it.

Returning to the hotel, I recall buying an ice-cream from an elderly lady in the street near the Metro exit. I couldn't help thinking how tough life must be to earn a living in such a way. The ice-cream was simply rolled in pieces of paper and piled in a basket. No freezer required. That purchase voluntarily set me back fifty times the asking price.

Early on the morning of the 6th December 1979, I bade farewell to Tonya. Suffice to say it was extremely emotional. Tonya came with me to the airport but remained in the taxi. I last saw her through the rear window as the taxi drove away but soon lost sight as snow was again falling.

Flight SU142 took off that morning at ten thirty-five bound for Heathrow. I don't remember the flight but arrived home at ten minutes to three. The welcome I received when I stepped through the door at Knebworth was overwhelming but my thoughts were still in Moscow......

Mission Accomplished

Chapter 47

Reality Check

My mission to Moscow had lasted just fifteen days but so much had happened in such a short time that a comparison with daily life at home left me feeling restless.

A telephone call to Cunard head office in London on the 7th of December was sufficient to confirm renewal of my contract and get me back on the payroll. It was a relief to me since I had been aware of the increasing number of redundancies within the company in the preceding months.

British merchant shipping was on the decline due to containerisation and cheaper transportation tariffs by foreign competitors. Many of my sea-going friends had already been made redundant and were looking to foreign shipping companies for employment or faced leaving the sea altogether as a career. There were dark days ahead.

That same afternoon I had a visit from Special Branch of Hertfordshire Constabulary. WDC June Lynch Interviewed me regarding my time in Russia. Perhaps Special Branch thought they may have a Russian spy on their doorstep. When I asked her if that was the case, she just smiled.

On the 9th of December I rode to Southampton on my Norton Commando motorcycle. It was cold and raining heavily for the entire one-hundred-and-five mile journey. I booked into the merchant navy hotel and overheard conversations in the foyer about the outside temperature. Cold? - these people had obviously not experienced a Russian winter!

The next day I had a 9am start at The School Of Navigation in Warsash. I had been booked on a tanker safety course for that week. I don't quite know why. I had only ever served on a tanker once before and had no intention of repeating the experience. Besides, Cunard had no remaining tankers. During that course, my mind was elsewhere. Tonya had asked me before I left Russia if I could send her some fashion magazines. Oh, and a picture postcard of the Queen. So I did.

My return home was met by newspaper reporters who had discovered the marriage through a small press announcement that my mum had placed without my knowledge. On three occasions during one week, separate newspapers hounded me for the story. I didn't mind at first but the intrusion persisted until I refused more interviews. I still have most of the cuttings.

Also at this time, I was in negotiation regarding a mortgage to be taken out on a flat in Hitchin. If Tonya was able to leave Russia and join me, we would need somewhere to live.

Christmas 1979 was spent at home in Knebworth. Quite a rare occasion really, as I had been at sea for most others since 1972. It was very pleasant to be home but of course there was an important individual absent which rather diluted the festivities for me. I wondered what Christmas was like in Novorossiysk for Tonya and her family.

January 1980 must have been a slack time for Cunard. Instead of joining my next ship, I was allotted placements on training courses.

The 6th of January found me riding to Lowestoft. Yet again it was raining and I arrived at my lodgings, St Francis House, after dark.

I had expected a hotel but these were lean times in the shipping industry. I was ushered to a large, damp and dingy room at the top of the house which I was to share with a colleague. I was given strict instructions by the conservative landlady that dinner would be at 7pm sharp and that bible classes would follow! My escape plan germinated.

Moving to the Royal George Hotel next day was the result of that plan. The Electronic Navigational Aids course that I attended was concluded by an examination at the end of the week.

The ride home on the Norton was in snow and bitter cold - I needed to upgrade my riding gear.

At long last, on the 16th of January, a letter arrived from Tonya. Despite my having written numerous letters, this was the first communication I had received from her since leaving Moscow. Disappointingly, there was no news on the progress of Tonya's exit visa application.

A Ship Master's Medical course in Liverpool was my next assignment starting on January 21st. Another examination at the end of the week and return home.

February arrived and on the 2nd, I flew to John F. Kennedy airport in New York. I was to join my next ship, Andria, in Galveston. For some undisclosed reason, I was detained by an immigration official and taken to a small room to await interview. I waited alone but became increasingly concerned that I may miss my connecting flight to Houston. After almost an hour, I ventured outside to find another immigration official. He couldn't explain why I had been detained and I was free to go. I had to race to another terminal and only just made the connection in time.

My only conclusion to this bizarre event was that Russian stamps in my passport may have alarmed the first American official. The Cold War had not yet begun to thaw.

Andria was a fruit ship. Refrigerated and built for speed, she was one of a class designed to deliver her cargoes as swiftly as possible to avoid deterioration of, in this case, bananas.

I joined the Andria in Galveston on the 4th of February and was to spend the next four months shipping bananas around the Americas.

After discharging cargo in Galveston there were no immediate plans for our next assignment so we took Andria to an anchorage at Cristobal, which is situated at the Atlantic end of the Panama Canal to await instructions.

For three days, Andria lay at anchor barely half a mile from the insect-infested coastline. Routine bridge watches had to be maintained and, due to the heat and humidity, the wheelhouse doors were kept wide open. Just before the change of watch at around midnight on the 10th of February, I was leaning over the chart table when I became aware that something was crawling up my back. I turned to look over my right shoulder and saw two long antennae slowly followed by a large, bug-eyed head. I froze but could feel sharp pin-pricks through my uniform shirt. At that moment, Charlie Bathgate, our Scottish Second Mate, came into the wheelhouse. He took one look at me and his eyes widened in horror.

"What is it Charlie?' I whispered.

"Ah dinna nae, ah hav'na seen anything like it before. Dinna move!" he replied before disappearing out of my sight.

Moments that seemed like ages later, he returned with a towel and with one almighty swipe, he whacked me on the back. A huge, beetle-like bug hit the wheelhouse floor and Charlie jumped on it. When he stood back we both looked at it in awe. It was a full six inches long and had a thick outer shell. It had long, spiked legs and pincers.

"That's the end of that wee beastie!" Charlie said. He was wrong, the bug began to move and it took two more hefty jumps to confirm its demise.

As the ship's meteorological and natural-science reporting officer, I preserved and sent the specimen, along with completed log books, to the Meteorological Office at Bracknell.

On my eventual return home, I was amazed to discover that I had been awarded a prize and certificate for my observation of a hitherto unrecorded insect variety. Perhaps the imprint of Charlie's tread pattern had confused the specialists!

Chapter 48

Reality Check 2

On the 14th of February 1980, Andria berthed in Santa Marta, a port on the north coast of Colombia. Laying along the same quayside was a Russian trawler. As there was no immediate cargo activity, I took the opportunity for a stroll, intending to see what lay beyond the dock gates.

On passing the trawler, I nodded to a crew man who was leaning on the boat's rail.

"Dobrey ootra" I said in my now well-practised accent.

He looked at me in astonishment."Ve gavareete pa Ruski, da?" he replied.

"Da, nymnoga - mya zhena eta Ruski" I continued as if I was a welcome comrade.

Anyway, as a result of our complex dialogue, other members of the trawler's crew soon appeared to investigate. It quickly became obvious to me that these Russians were interested to know if Andria was well supplied with scotch whisky. I was offered bottles of vodka if an exchange was possible. I was able to communicate that I would see what I could do.

That afternoon I returned to the trawler with two bottles of Bell's scotch. I was welcomed aboard as if I had been wearing a Santa costume. Below deck there was a tiny kitchen area with a table and bench seats on either side. I was invited to sit down and was quickly surrounded on all sides by crewmen eager not to miss out on a sample or two of western decadence.

Now I don't happen to drink whisky, but I had become accustomed to vodka from previous experience. Perhaps it was just as well, since I didn't want to offend my hosts. Russians like to drink and within half an hour only a drop of whisky was left. Bottles of vodka were pushed in my direction and it was clear that further consignments of Bell's would be most welcome.

All the trawler crew were now on friendly terms and when I was asked about Tonya, I explained as best I could about the lack of communication with her since leaving Moscow. One of the crew passed a blank piece of paper across the table and asked me to write down her place of work. I was a little suspicious and asked the reason. After looking at the note, he explained that he was the radio operator and may be able to make contact with the Novorossiysk Shipping Head Office. The working day had just begun there and he was proud to add that his transmitter was extremely powerful.

The radio operator got up from the table and left. Our merry group continued to demolish the remaining scotch before following it with vodka. I must admit I was feeling every bit as merry as the Russians and began making my excuses to leave. The Russians seemed genuinely sorry to see me go but I indicated that I would try to return with further supplies before Andria left port.

As I stood up I was offered more vodka bottles than I could carry, but elected just one as a souvenir. I made for the doorway just as the radio operator was returning. He had made contact with a Tonya Kumyetz. Was there a message I wanted to send?

The message he sent was brief but that didn't matter - it was a real time communication from the other side of the world from a source that could not have been matched anywhere.

I know that Tonya was as surprised to receive a message from me as I was to send it. It was a very special opportunity - but then after all - it was Saint Valentine's Day!

Walking the short distance back to Andria got me thinking. I turned to look back at the trawler. For such a small vessel it had an extraordinary number of radio aerials. Trawlers usually smelled strongly of fish but this one didn't. I had heard that the Russians operated a fleet of small vessels used in the Cold War spying game. Could this be one of them?

Part loaded with bananas, Andria departed Santa Marta during the afternoon of the 15th of February. Before leaving, I deposited two more bottles of Bell's with the trawler crew but declined another invitation aboard. A minor triumph for Anglo-Soviet relations however, had been achieved.

For the following month, Andria plied her trade between the banana producing countries of Central America and the banana eating states of North America. Contrary to popular belief, the seas of the Caribbean and Gulf of Mexico can be extremely hazardous. More often than not, we would encounter heavy weather with resulting torrential rain and huge waves. The Andria's sleek design had the major drawback that she would pitch and roll alarmingly in a rough sea.

On the 9th of March, Andria left the port of Almirante bound for Bremmerhaven in Northern Germany. Obviously, this meant crossing the North Atlantic Ocean at an unpredictable time of year. I navigated the ship through The Windward Passage on my morning watch of the 11th of March and almost immediately ran into a heavy sea.

For the next ten days, life aboard was exhausting. Andria was not built for the weather we encountered. The ship would rise on a mountainous swell and then plunge into a trough, burying the bow in water. Simultaneously, she would roll so violently that each crew member wondered if she would return upright. When off-duty, sleep was virtually impossible and meals became an art to manage. Our Captain instructed that no one should venture on deck except in an extreme emergency. For much of that voyage, Andria behaved more like a submarine than a surface vessel. It was a passage I shall never forget and am extremely pleased to have survived in order to remember those ten days.

Chapter 49

Exodus

A ndria's discharge in Bremmerhaven on the 22nd of March 1980 lasted just 24 hours. My 26th birthday had been spent weathering storm conditions in the Western Approaches and I had hoped a longer stay in Germany would compensate. Instead, it was back to the Caribbean and Central America for more yellow gold - bananas were making a welcome profit for the company.

Fully laden at Turbo and Almirante, we crossed the Atlantic once again but this time our discharge ports included Oslo as well as Bremmerhaven. On this occasion we had more time to spend discovering as much of the local areas as time permitted.

Another trans-Atlantic passage took us to Tela in Honduras and Kingston in Jamaica. By now the sea had moderated to make our time steaming between ports tolerable.

On the 18th of May, Andria passed through Crooked Island Passage among the Bahamas and began, what was for me, a homeward bound voyage - although I didn't know it yet.

Arrival in Bremmerhaven on the 28th was frenetic. Discharge began immediately on arrival and, no sooner had I opened the deck cargo hatches, I was informed that my relief had arrived on board and my flight home booked for the following day. This allowed time to handover to the new Third Mate whilst assisting with all the activity on deck.

That evening was spent in a pleasant local hotel celebrating release with the other Andria personnel who were going home on leave. In contrast to other ships, no one regretted leaving Andria.

At midday on the 29th of May I arrived home. During my time away, ownership of the flat in Hitchin had been confirmed and I was keen to make it into a home. However, I spent my first couple of leave days at Knebworth with parents, adjusting back to life on dry land and beginning the search for flat furnishings.

June was spent making number 3 Woodcote House in Queen Street, Hitchin, as comfortable as funds would allow. Apart from savings made during my time aboard Andria, funds were scarce due to expenses incurred in Russia.

Unexpectedly, the head of the Schreiber furniture empire heard of my recent ventures and, as a result, sent me his latest catalogue along with a letter allowing me one thousand pound's worth of Schreiber furniture as a wedding gift. In 1980, that sum was sufficient to buy all the essentials.

I had met Mr Schreiber only once, way back in 1973 during my adventure to Israel. He had offered me a position in his company at that time, but I politely declined as it could not compete with the life I was living aboard the QE2.

On the 4th of June, I visited The Foreign Office in London as well as my company head office in Hammersmith. I collected letters numbered 15 and 16 from Tonya. For the first time there was a positive accent in her writing. Still no firm news regarding a visa but nothing negative either.

The news I had been waiting for finally arrived on the 13th. Tonya had been granted an exit visa!

Superstition? - this was the best news we'd had since the evening I spent in Sochi discussing our dilemma with the manageress of Hotel Kamelia back in November of the previous year.

Our big day materialised on Wednesday, the 2nd of July 1980 when I travelled to Heathrow Airport to meet Tonya who was due to arrive on Flight SU 124. I was waiting in the arrivals foyer when I saw her emerge from the customs exit. She appeared apprehensive until she caught sight of me and then a smile replaced the anxious look. Hugs quickly followed, although I had learned that Russians rarely display emotion in public. At that time it really didn't matter. What mattered most was that at last all our plans had matured and Tonya had finally made her journey to the west.

Travelling home by underground and train was charged with excitement. Tonya's English had improved way beyond my mastery of Russian, so I gallantly agreed to speak only in English from now on. The Penguin phrase book was officially retired.

Tonya had so many questions that we were back in Knebworth before I could answer them all.

I was now able to introduce Tonya to my mum and dad for the first time. Both parents took over asking her questions so that I could hardly get a word in of my own. We all had dinner together and talked until late. My mum then insisted that we both spend the night there.

Next day I introduced Tonya to our one bed flat in Hitchin. I had hoped she wasn't expecting an Englishman's castle. Russian literature frequently refers to the perceived Englishman and his landed way of life, including his castle. She reassured me that a hut would be sufficient as we were together. It pleased me to hear that - castles were in rather short supply.

So began a new life for both of us.

Chapter 50

New Horizons

For Tonya, everything about her new life was in deep contrast to the one she had just left behind.

Supermarket and department store shopping, western television, radio and cinema, even eating out at an Indian restaurant, were all fresh experiences.

Thursday, 17th July 1980, was marked by a detailed article in the Stevenage Gazette newspaper under the heading 'Love lifts the Iron Curtain' and announcing the arrival of Tonya into the U.K.

The National press quickly jumped on the bandwagon with financial incentives to run the story, but Tonya was adamant she didn't want further publicity. Her reasoning was that if any adverse comments regarding Soviet bureaucracy appeared in print, it could cause problems for her family back home. Although the local press had printed several articles, including a front page story since December, no further coverage followed.

On the 11th of August 1980, application was made to The Home Office for Tonya's registration. At this time, a foreign national could expect to wait five years before becoming a British subject, even if they were married to one. In the meantime, Tonya could only travel on her Russian passport and this would cause major problems in the months ahead.

Those months ahead included joining container ships in Tilbury for short runs to the continent and back. My contract with Cunard allowed for Tonya to accompany me - which was just as well since she had no contacts in the U.K. and her English was still very basic.

Amsterdam, Hamburg and Rotterdam were regular ports of call but usually only allowed time for brief visits ashore. However, from the 25th of August to the 15th of September, my container ship, named ACT 2, was placed in a dry dock in Amsterdam. Container ships, by virtue of their ability to load or discharge their cargoes quickly, don't usually spend long periods in port, so this presented a rare opportunity to tour the city thoroughly. Having had that opportunity, I now consider Amsterdam to be one of the most impressive cities I have ever visited.

After time spent aboard ACT 2 and then her sister ship, ACT 6, I had a short period of home leave before journeying on an overnight train to Falmouth. So, on the 24th of November, Tonya and I boarded Port Caroline for some proper seafaring. There was much to do before this ship was ready to put to sea. She had been laid up in the River Fal along with her sister, Port Chalmers, and had suffered neglect. My first priority was to ensure all safety equipment was intact along with lifeboats and emergency provisions as we were rumoured to be bound for South Africa.

In the event, we departed Falmouth that same day en route to Marseilles to load fruit for ports in The Middle East. Once out at sea, it became apparent that Tonya was susceptible to sea-sickness. The weather in The Channel worsened as we entered The Bay of Biscay and remained rough until we berthed in the south of France. Worryingly, Tonya was severely ill for the entire passage. It was a portent of what lay ahead and an extremely unfortunate way to spend our first wedding anniversary.

On the 1st of December, whilst still in Marseilles, I was promoted to the rank of Second Mate. This hallowed position carried extra responsibilities. I was now the chief navigating officer and third in line to command the largest refrigerated ship in the world. Port Caroline was also the flagship of the famous Port Line fleet. Sleep came slowly that night.

Four days later, Port Caroline slipped her moorings and headed out into The Mediterranean Sea eastward bound for Port Said. This was my first passage as the ship's navigator and I spent long periods studying charts and double checking our position. Noon positions had to be calculated from sextant readings coupled with chronometer timings. Although I had done this many times before, I wanted to leave no room for error. Our first landfall would be the low-lying Egyptian coast with few recognisable landmarks, so I needed to be accurate in order to arrive with port buildings in sight rather than just sand dunes.

My calculations tied in with the first radar echoes of Port Said and I breathed a sigh of great relief. The Suez Canal transit was tricky due to an incredibly strong cross wind. It was decided to moor up. In my opinion, our captain made the wrong decision to tie the ship to the windward bank of the canal to wait out the conditions. We should have allowed ourselves to drift to leeward and moored on the opposite bank. My job was to secure the after end of the ship. In the event, I was instructed to put too much weight on the after mooring lines. This endangered my deck party as well as myself, since a parting mooring line can be lethal. As a result, the operation was a failure and the ship was stuck in mid-channel for many hours with all deck crew kept unnecessarily at their stations. The airborne sand hitting exposed eyes and skin was literally torturous.

That captain didn't last. He had been desk-bound for too long prior to this command and it showed. Fortunately for us, he was relieved shortly after this incident. I shall not forget his name.

From Suez we called in at Jeddah on the Saudi west coast and then on to Kuwait where we berthed on Christmas day. Arabs must have liked our apples since Port Caroline returned to Marseilles for another full cargo, returning to Kuwait on the 12th of February 1981.

After our second discharge at Kuwait, we received instructions to proceed to Port Elizabeth and Cape Town in South Africa where more fruit was loaded for Europe. This passage down the East African coast was made in a calm sea but Tonya continued to suffer sea-sickness at the slightest movement.

Whilst in Cape Town we had some unexpected free time due to a labour dispute among the South African cargo handlers. On one of our trips ashore, I got talking to a diamond merchant with the result that we were invited to stay overnight with his family inland at Somerset West. So we did. Another opportunity took us by cable car to the summit of Table Mountain. I had made this pilgrimage on a previous visit but of course, Tonya had not, so when in Cape Town......

On leaving South Africa on the 25th of March, I laid a course on the ship's chart which would take us across the Great African Bight to make landfall just east of Gran Canaria. This would be our longest passage out of sight of land and all seemed well until the day of our expected landfall. Now Gran Canaria is an ancient volcanic island rising more than six thousand feet above sea level. On a clear day, the island would be seen from about fifty miles distant on the approach. Even further if abnormal refraction was present. At this time, I reckoned we were within fifty miles.

So there I was in the wheelhouse along with our replacement captain to observe the sighting. Naturally, this was a big moment for me as navigator. Had I made all the correct navigational calculations? We would soon find out. An hour passed - Nothing. Both the captain and I were now on the port bridge wing and straining with binoculars to see the first sight of land. Still nothing.

"Well, where are we two-oh?" Captain Croall asked rather impatiently.

"Should see the mountain at any time now, sir" I replied whilst trying to sound positive.

More time passed. Still nothing. I went to the chart, checked our expected position and calculated the island to be within ten miles. Blimey! we'll soon be on top of it! Had I made a calamitous error? Back on the bridge wing, the captain was pacing and beginning to look worried. I felt the same but didn't want to alarm him further. All I could do was take another look through my binoculars, although this should't have been necessary at such close range.

Still nothing at sea level, but as I looked upwards with a feeling of despair, I saw the most magnificent sight. There, above cloud level was the massive Pico de las Nieves. We were bang on target! I strolled over to Captain Croall and just pointed skywards.

"Well bu**er me!" he simply said.

Haze at sea is an odd phenomena. At sea level, even on a clear day, it can reduce visibility to alarming levels. Today we were experiencing such phenomena. Port Caroline was dwarfed by the volcano causing us to stare skywards. It is another one of those sights that remains lodged in my memory. That morning I felt rather pleased with myself as I adjusted our gyro compass and set a new course for home.

Chapter 51

Altering Course

Port Caroline arrived in Antwerp on 11th of April 1981. After discharging most of her cargo of Cape fruit, she was made ready to put to sea again. I went up to the wheelhouse where I laid off my final course on the North Sea chart for passage to Hull. We had been notified that most of the ship's company would be going home on leave when we berthed, but I had no idea at this time how the next few months would unfold.

Leaving that magnificent ship in Hull on the afternoon of Thursday, 16th of April 1981 was to be the end of an era. The sad reality was that all traditional, freight-carrying ships were being replaced by container ships of ever increasing size. Port Caroline was simply obsolete.

Cunard's fleet, which included the last of the Port Line ships, was being drastically reduced in size. Consequently, so were the crews needed to operate them. I was lucky, I had been aware of company redundancies for some considerable time but still remained on the payroll.

So Tonya and I travelled back to Hitchin. I know that Tonya was quite relieved to be on dry land again, because it was clear by now that she was unlikely to overcome her chronic sea-sickness.

I had several weeks of leave to take and began a pleasant routine, visiting friends and family, shopping and improving our flat. I resumed rallying with my Norton while Tonya took up yoga.

Cunard's plans for my future remained uncertain and even a visit to our head office on the 30th of April shed little light. I did see a list of officers who had been made redundant that month and so enquired about next month's list but the reply was vague. I left the building with a feeling that time was being borrowed.

The press were still active and on 5th May, The Hitchin Express ran a follow up story on our progress. The headline 'From Russia With Love' lacked imagination but the reporter had told us that even minor comments like Tonya's discovery of cornflakes was what the readership found interesting. I still have all the newspaper cuttings from this period.

Cunard must have valued my services more than I had anticipated, because they saw fit to place me on a radar simulator course at The City Of London Polytechnic starting on the 18th of May.

I had already applied to sit the Board Of Trade first mate's examination and saw this course as a stepping stone.

The radar course was followed by a Cunard officer's seminar at The Cambridgeshire Hotel on the 29th. Not surprisingly, the main topic of conversation was centered around the future of the company and its employees. Quite a few of those present had already made application to join foreign-flag shipping companies that were still recruiting British officers holding a Board Of Trade qualification. Some of those companies were paying higher salaries too. All very tempting.

Crunch time came on the 10th of June when, following a letter of invitation, I attended our head office in Hammersmith to learn that the inevitable had arrived. I was complimented on my service to Cunard, and offered a redundancy package that would keep the wolves from the door for barely three months. The package fell far short of what would have been due had I not ended my previous contract in order to return to Russia. Marriage comes at financial loss to many.

The dilemma facing me now was to consider applying to a foreign-flag shipping company or look in another direction. I now had a mortgage to pay and a young wife who was solely dependent on me. Taking into consideration Tonya's chronic sea-sickness, I felt I had little choice but to search for a new career on shore. But where to start?

A year earlier, whilst waiting for Tonya's arrival to the U.K., I had applied to the Royal Air Force for consideration to join their marine division. I knew they operated high-speed rescue launches as far afield as Gan Island in the Indian Ocean and that appealed to me. The position, pending final interview at Biggin Hill, was virtually in the bag until I enquired if it would make much difference if I was married to a Soviet citizen. It took two full weeks for the R.A.F. to confirm that it probably would!

I considered that someone having been employed in a disciplined, uniformed organisation may be suitable for a police career, so I applied to Hertfordshire Constabulary. During my initial telephone call I felt almost dissuaded by the recruitment office by being informed that only a tiny number of applicants are successful and in any case the waiting list for interview was at least a year.

So I applied anyway - along with other career avenues. In the meantime, I took a job as a motorcycle courier with Dixon's Despatch of Stevenage. This work was fun to begin with but I was never going to make my fortune as a despatch rider, no matter how many hours I put in. The work could be dangerous too. Twice I took a tumble on London's North Circular Road. Fortunately, I had bought a very second-hand Honda 400cc motorbike for this work, saving my beloved Norton from the resulting knocks and scrapes.

British Aerospace offered me a position in their missile-building empire, but it involved flying a desk and that just didn't appeal. Besides, contrary to earlier information received, I was invited for formal interview at Hertfordshire Police Headquarters on Tuesday, the 13th of October - months before I had expected to hear anything.

Nine candidates had been invited for interview on that day. The nine were told on arrival that they were the result of a paper-sift of more than one hundred recent applicants. The interviews took all day with a short break for lunch. All nine were confident and hopeful, but at the day's end, only two had proved successful.

I was one of them.